PRAISE FOR *H3 LEADERSHIP*

"Brad Lomenick has dedicated himself to a noble quest: helping young people become great leaders. There is no better path to social improvement than deploying legions of exceptional leaders into the teeth of our most-pressing problems, all the better if they're young enough to be undaunted, with decades of opportunity for contribution ahead of them."

Jim Collins, author *Good to Great*

"Lead yourself. How can you attempt to lead others until you embrace this simple truth? Brad Lomenick is one of the good guys, and he's generously sharing what he's learned in his own journey."

Seth Godin, author, *The Icarus Deception*

"A few key 'H' words have been used to create the strong foundation of his philosophy and book, yet the one I think of most when I think of Brad is 'honest.' It takes real honesty, self-analysis and reflection to truly become a great leader and to discuss leadership in such a new and compelling way."

Blake Mycoskie, founder and chief shoe giver, TOMS

"Looking to put your leadership into action? Look no further than H3 Leadership. Put this book to good use. It's loaded with application and real-time, real-life leadership."

John Maxwell, #1 *New York Times* bestselling author

"Hungry. Humble. Hustle. Those three words are Brad Lomenick's mantra, and they characterize just about every quality, hard-charging, effective leader I know. When it comes to Brad's *H3 Leadership*, though, I'd add one more H: HOW. This book is your how-to when it comes to leading your organization. Don't miss it."

Dave Ramsey, *New York Times* bestselling author and nationally syndicated radio show host

"Hustle, hungry, humble—the three H's in H3—is the formula for successful leadership as discovered by Brad Lomenick. By making leadership a habit—twenty habits, in fact—you'll become a better leader, a better person, and someone who is more deeply in touch with spiritual principles. This is a great read for anyone at any stage of their leadership journey."

Daniel H. Pink, author of *Drive* and *To Sell Is Human*

"*H3 Leadership* makes a case for every leader, at every level, to push the boundaries by living out Brad's mantra: Humble, Hungry, and Hustle. A triple threat that makes leadership better and last longer."

Soledad O'Brien

"Leadership can be one of the most difficult journeys for any person to take. Let Brad Lomenick be your guide."

Simon Sinek, bestselling author

"Don't just read this book- consume it, retain it, and implement it in your daily life. Allow Brad to be your leadership guru and strategic advisor. You won't regret it."

Mark Burnett, CEO, United Artists Media Group; Award-winning executive producer of *The Voice, Shark Tank, Survivor,* and *The Bible*

"For years, Brad has been a leader of leaders. How? He's always been humble, he's always stayed hungry and he's always hustled. I've personally learned a lot from Brad about leadership, and in this book the rest of the world can too. Read it!"

Jon Acuff, *New York Times* bestselling author of *Do Over: Rescue Monday, Reinvent Your Work and Never Get Stuck*

"A practical resource for leaders at all levels."

Adam Grant, Wharton professor and *New York Times* bestselling author of *Give and Take*

"If you want to take your leadership to the next level, read this book. *H3 Leadership* is a practical handbook on everyday influence. It's a game changer and will adequately fuel your leadership journey, regardless of where you are in the process."

Charlene Li, Author of *Engaged Leader and New York Times* bestseller *Open Leadership*

"What I like about *H3 Leadership* was Brad's willingness to hit the reset button and rethink his leadership. What I love is his willingness to share his findings. Wow. What a trove of insights and discoveries. Catalyst grew like crazy under Brad's vision. Now we can too."

Michael Hyatt, blogger, MichaelHyatt.com; *New York Times* bestselling author of *Platform: Get Noticed in a Noisy World*

"We've said around our office for years that what we look for in new team members is "humble and hungry." I'm on the same page as Brad related to the idea and practice of *H3 Leadership,* and you should be too. This book is a helpful road map for living out your leadership in a tangible, daily way. For a small business owner like myself intent on continuing to grow my organization, this book is incredibly valuable and close to my desk for reference."

Donald Miller, bestselling author

"If you're looking for practical leadership wisdom, you've found it with *H3 Leadership.* Do a cannonball with your leadership journey and jump in feet first! Brad's perspective, experience, and expertise makes him the right voice to have as your leadership mentor. I enthusiastically recommend this book!"

Bob Goff, *New York Times* bestselling author of *Love Does*

"Written with great care and wisdom, Lomenick empowers the next generation of leaders with the tools to run the race well and finish strong. This book is essential reading for those who want to develop habits of success in leadership."

Gary A. Haugen, President and CEO of International Justice Mission, author of *The Locust Effect*

"Practical. Purposeful. Proven. *H3 Leadership* is a winner. Buy this book, read it, then read it again."

Nancy Duarte, author of *Resonate*

"If you're a leader, then *H3 Leadership* has something for you. Hustle, Hungry, Humble. I like all of these 3 H's as a simple but powerful model of Leadership. To me, the most important of the three today is a humble spirit brought to your leadership approach. Great book to pick up, read it, and keep it on the shelf for continual reference!"

Pat Gelsinger, CEO of VMware and former Chief Technology Officer, Intel

"I've known Brad for almost twenty years and have seen this leadership mantra lived out. *H3 Leadership* will help you start strong, end strong, and enjoy the journey. A great resource for leaders looking to lead well, and lead now."

Bill Haslam, Governor of Tennessee

"Hustle. Hungry. Humble. Those are three things I want to be and traits I want to have as a leader. And you should too. A triple threat that will not only make your leadership better but will make your leadership last. So read this book!"

Christine Caine, speaker, bestselling author, and founder of the A21 Campaign

"Brad Lomenick strikes again with another book leaders shouldn't miss. You'll definitely strive to make the three "H's" a part of your daily diet after reading this book."

Scott Harrison, founder and CEO, charity: water

"I highly recommend Hustle, Hungry, Humble to the leader that desires to intentionally take their leadership to the next level. Brad Lomenick has brilliantly developed the three H's from wisdom gained from his own journey over the past 20 years. I believe H3 is a game changer and will definitely inspire, challenge and sustain you on your leadership journey."

Aja Brown, honorable mayor of Compton, California

H3 LEADERSHIP

BE HUMBLE. STAY HUNGRY. ALWAYS HUSTLE.

Brad Lomenick

NELSON
BOOKS

An Imprint of Thomas Nelson

Published in Nashville, Tennessee, by Nelson Books, an imprint of Thomas Nelson. Nelson Books and Thomas Nelson are registered trademarks of HarperCollins Christian Publishing, Inc.

The author is represented by Christopher Ferebee, Attorney and Literary Agent, www. christopherferebee.com.

Thomas Nelson, Inc., titles may be purchased in bulk for educational, business, fund-raising, or sales promotional use. For information, please e-mail SpecialMarkets@ThomasNelson.com.

Unless otherwise indicated, Scripture quotations are taken from the Holy Bible, New International Version`, NIV`. Copyright © 1973, 1978, 1984, 2011 by Biblica, Inc.™ Used by permission. All rights reserved worldwide.

Scripture quotations marked ESV are from the ESV® Bible (The Holy Bible, English Standard Version®). Copyright © 2001 by Crossway, a publishing ministry of Good News Publishers. Used by permission. All rights reserved.

Scripture quotations marked KJV are from the King James Version. Public domain.

Scripture quotations marked NASB are from the NEW AMERICAN STANDARD BIBLE®, © The Lockman Foundation 1960, 1962, 1963, 1968, 1971, 1972, 1973, 1975, 1977, 1995. Used by permission.

Library of Congress Control Number: 2015937979

ISBN-13: 978-0-7180-2225-9
ISBN-13: 978-0-7180-7793-8 (IE)

Printed in the United States of America

16 17 18 19 RRD 6 5 4 3 2

CONTENTS

FOREWORD

Many people know me as the executive producer of hit television shows like *The Voice, Shark Tank, Celebrity Apprentice,* and one of the longest-running shows on TV, *Survivor.* Some assume life has always been easy for me.

People return my calls now, but not so long ago I couldn't get anyone to respond to me. I now get pitched new shows constantly, but not so long ago I couldn't get anyone to listen to my ideas. Point is—this has been a marathon, not a sprint. My success today was built and developed through the nitty-gritty grind of thirty years of hard work, sweat, perseverance, a willing spirit, and relentless pursuit of the goal. My life journey has taken me from the military in the UK, to landing with nothing but dreams and a whole lot of hustle in Hollywood some twenty-five years ago, to now stewarding an ever-expanding entertainment company, with hopefully many more hit shows and dreams to be achieved in the coming years.

The overall journey and process has definitely defined me.

I'm no overnight success. Humble, hungry, and hustle accurately describe some of the qualities that got me to where I am.

When I look back at my leadership journey, a critical part of it was the mentors, friends, and wise counsel who have helped me along the way. Which is why I'm so excited about this book.

I first met Brad Lomenick four years ago at an event in Washington, DC. I was there to speak and connect with fifty or so key influential leaders in the faith community. After chatting a bit, Brad mentioned he was leading a movement of young leaders called Catalyst and asked me to speak at LA's Catalyst West in 2011. Roma and I had just announced what would go on to become one of the most-watched miniseries ever on cable television, *The Bible*, so I was excited to speak to a roomful of Christian leaders from across industries about our project. I'm not quite sure what I expected at the time, but I was blown away by the Catalyst conference and jokingly referred to it as the MTV Music Awards of the Christian community. It was high energy, excellent at every level, young and vibrant, and I felt like I was among friends. I was blown away by the quality of the leaders in attendance. It had been a while since I'd seen something described as Christian or faith-based that had such a strong and powerful edge to it. This was a movement, a tribe, a true community.

Brad has today broadened his areas of expertise beyond running Catalyst, and in *H3 Leadership* he's still helping people build their leadership platform by focusing on twenty key leadership habits that will teach you to be a better, stronger leader.

Leadership matters. Your leadership matters. A good leader changes the course of organizations, entire industries, states, countries, and even the global landscape.

I'm honored to introduce you to a book that will not only help you lead now, but will help you lead well.

Don't just read this book—consume it, retain it, and implement it in your daily life. Allow Brad Lomenick to be your leadership guide, guru, and strategic advisor. You won't regret it.

Mark Burnett
Chief Executive Officer, United Artists Media Group
Award-winning executive producer of *The Voice*,
Shark Tank, *Survivor*, and *The Bible*
Malibu, California
2015

LET THE TRANSFORMATION BEGIN

There comes a moment in the life of every leader when he or she stands at a crossroads and must ask, "What's next?" This moment for me came in October 2013, when I realized I was personally, professionally, physically, and spiritually burned-out.

The fire of my passion had been red-hot for years during my tenure as president of Catalyst. Our team had grown the organization into a premier conference and content provider for emerging and established leaders. Tens of thousands were participating in our events across the country, hundreds of thousands more were engaging with our content online, and we were making preparations for our first international gathering.

Yet, each morning that I walked into the office, I felt I had less to give than the day before. Less energy. Less creativity. Less passion. Less patience. I was running on fumes, with no filling station in view. My leadership was getting stale, and those closest to me were suffering as a result.

I needed a break, but didn't even realize it.

One day in late summer would be a turning point. It was August 10.

I had planned a lunch with a friend named Steve Cockram. We had some surface conversation, then Steve dove deep, asking if I was still passionate about leading Catalyst for the next decade.

After stammering, I admitted I was tired and wrung out.

Steve responded that he had sensed that for some time. He compared me to a heavyweight boxer who is still fighting in the fifteenth round, with no desire to bow out, but is just getting pounded. Throwing in the towel—transitioning out of my role—felt like admitting I was a loser. I wasn't going to do that. At the same time I felt stuck, and that wasn't fun either.

My conversation with Steve continued over the next couple of weeks before he finally dropped the big one on me: "Brad, you need a sabbatical. And you need to take it soon."

I rolled my eyes at the idea. *Sabbaticals are for college professors and old people*, I thought. But with some more thought, I began to realize that Steve was right. I was having a leadership crisis and needed to gain some perspective.

Seated at my desk in the Catalyst headquarters, I pulled up a new document on my computer and began sketching out plans for an extended sabbatical. I started with the basics: I would travel, reflect, relax, read, and establish a consistent physical exercise schedule. I wanted to re-center myself spiritually, spending more time in prayer, Bible study, and soaking up wisdom from my mentors. The excitement grew with each keystroke.

I announced the decision to my team a week later, and their reactions confirmed my decision. They felt that time away was necessary, having watched from afar as the edges of my life frayed. The Brad they had once seen engaging his work with a fresh resolve each morning was fading into a memory, replaced by someone they liked far less.

Over the next four months I executed my sabbatical plans with precision. I traveled to London to spend time with a spiritual

LET THE TRANSFORMATION BEGIN

adviser and friend and to Guatemala in partnership with a relief and development organization. I read dozens of books. I prayed a lot—and listened. I reconnected with friends. I spent time with family in Oklahoma. And of course I had to make a stop at the Rocky Mountains in Colorado and Lost Valley Ranch to recharge and relax.

Along the way, I was coming back to life. But something unforeseen was emerging. I began to have a creeping intuition that I was entering a new season altogether, that it was time to move on from the work I was doing and probe God's vision for the next stage of my life.

|||||||||||||||||||||||||||||||||||||||||||||||||||||||||||||||||||||||||||||||||||||||||||||||||||||||||||||||||||||||||||||||||||||||||||||||||||||||||||||||||||||||||

Every year I was at Catalyst, a new crop of interns would arrive on the scene, wide-eyed and eager. Their nervousness reflected the seriousness of their task. They'd been handed an opportunity to make their mark with the largest network of young Christian leaders in America.

I gathered them in my office for an orientation of sorts where I laid out the philosophy of our organization and the eight essentials of a "Catalyst leader." After I finished and before they began work, I always gave them the opportunity to ask me any questions they might have. Most years, one of the bolder and more aggressive of the bunch would raise his or her hand and ask the one question I knew would be coming:

"What do *we* need to do to become the kind of leader you're describing?"

Without hesitation I always replied, "Remember three words: *humble, hungry, hustle.*"

It was time to take my own advice. My leadership crisis required that I return to what I knew as a leader, beginning with my faith in Jesus and walk with God. That was and is foundational. But I also needed to revisit the three H's of leadership: *humble, hungry,* and *hustle.* I needed to reboot my leadership by putting these habits back in place.

Leaders will develop a variety of habits throughout their lives, but these three words divide them into categories that help answer three of the most important questions every influencer must ask:

- HUMBLE: "Who am I?"
- HUNGRY: "Where do I want to go?"
- HUSTLE: "How will I get there?"

This alliterated trio has become my personal life mantra over the last decade because it encapsulates the philosophy that undergirds what I believe it takes to become a change agent in the modern world. Leading is difficult, and anyone who has been in a position of authority or influence for very long knows this. It's hard work. But leadership is more than hard work; it is *habitual* work. It is worked out every day in the tasks we complete, the ways we approach our work, and the rhythms we nurture in our lives. It hangs on the hooks of the patterns we create, not just the success we may stumble upon.

> **LEADERSHIP IS MORE THAN HARD WORK; IT IS HABITUAL WORK.**

In my experience too few leaders recognize the importance of habits in life. One researcher at Duke University, for example, found that more than 40 percent of the actions people performed each day weren't actual decisions, but habits.[1] When you rise in the morning, nearly half of your day will be determined by the patterns you've either intentionally created or passively allowed.

I've had the privilege of working with the best and most respected leaders in America, and almost all of them share a common set of characteristics. They are principled and passionate, courageous and capable, hopeful and authentic, called and collaborative. But that leaves us with a lingering question: *How did they get there?* The path to being a better leader is paved with the asphalt of the habits we develop.

I think of my friend Lisa, who is a two-time *New York Times* bestselling author. I recently asked her how she created the magic with her books. "What most people don't know," she said, "is that I wrote multiple books before these that didn't sell well." She is like my friends who have a band that is becoming very successful. They recently performed on the *Today* show and their music has appeared in major companies' commercials, but they worked for years to put out several EPs that went largely unnoticed. In both cases it took time and hard work to develop the habits necessary to get better at their craft.

Or you might consider Kyle, a friend of mine who pastors a church that runs more than fifteen thousand in weekly attendance. For the first five years the congregation couldn't even pay their bills. Kyle considered getting out of the ministry altogether because he was so discouraged. But today, he shepherds the largest church in their denomination and has launched several successful satellite locations. He'll tell you that creating and sustaining better habits made all the difference.

Patterns are even crucial in sports, as Super Bowl–winning coach Tony Dungy can tell you. When he began coaching professional football, most people believed that teams needed thick playbooks full of unique and complex schemes. But Dungy took the opposite approach. He wanted to simplify the game to reduce the chance of error.

Rather than drilling hundreds of formations into his players' heads, he selected only a handful. But he made his team practice them relentlessly until the behaviors became second nature. Dungy was able to create faster, sleeker teams that ran on the fuel of habits. Often, the other team knew exactly which play his team was going to run when they lined up. But they couldn't overcome it because they couldn't keep up.

"Here are the six reasons everyone thinks we can't win," Dungy told the Tampa Bay Buccaneers after becoming head coach in 1996. He then listed everything the sportswriters and commentators had been saying: injuries among some of their better players, dysfunctional management, a new coach, spoiled players, a weak fan base, and a shallow roster.

> 🐦 **NEARLY HALF OF YOUR DAY WILL BE DETERMINED BY THE PATTERNS YOU'VE EITHER INTENTIONALLY CREATED OR PASSIVELY ALLOWED.**

"Those are the supposed reasons," Dungy said. "Now here is the fact: Nobody is going to outwork us."[2]

He knew that winning in the game of football takes more than better talent. It takes better habits. Tony Dungy went on to have much success with the Buccaneers, and later, with the Indianapolis Colts, with whom he would win the Super Bowl.

In 1994, a Harvard study examined people who had made significant changes in their lives. Researchers found that the impetus for change varied. Some had suffered a tragedy, others had witnessed a friend experience something awful and had learned from it, and still others changed because of social pressure. But while the reasons for their change varied, the constant among them was that their habits had shifted.[3]

There's no avoiding it: the patterns we cultivate shape the person we each become.

Unfortunately, most people aren't intentional about the habits they're developing. Our schedules or workloads or coworkers or environments often dictate our lives' patterns, and we end up leading reactively rather than proactively. You must develop habits that create consistency.

Life is about decisions. If you want to change, make a decision. Decisions build habits.

Habits take an idea and convert it into results. A habit is a practice shaped by behavior or daily action that helps turn ideals into action, principles into practice, and concepts into concrete. Habits allow for someone to actually implement ideas that last into his or her life. Leadership for the long haul comes from implementing regular, daily practices into your leadership journey. Habits create standard operating procedures in your life and are the fuel to get to the finish line.

Want to change? Create habits in your life. Want to be a better leader? Establish leadership habits. If you want to get better, work at it. Want to throw a football with a tighter spiral? Practice. Want to be a better putter in golf? Cultivate a habit of putting every night. Want to lose weight? Start eating well every day. Want to row the Atlantic Ocean? Row for several months in advance to build up the habits that will sustain you in the open seas. Habits create sustainable action out of chaotic energy.

🐦 **THE PATTERNS WE CULTIVATE SHAPE THE PERSON WE EACH BECOME.**

The reason too few leaders invest energy into developing better habits is that so many leaders have so little energy to invest in changing them. "Habit is a very powerful force that makes organizations get stuck doing things the same way over and over again," executive and bestselling author Patty Azzarello wrote in *Fast Company*. "Habits become ingrained (good and bad ones). And then everyone gets too over-busy to think about how there might be a better way to do something."[4]

Our work and friends and families can stretch us thin, and habits are not easy to create. Someone once told me that it takes about thirty days to create a habit. But this is false. Research has demonstrated that if you want to develop a habit of doing fifty sit-ups after morning coffee, for example, it will take as many as eighty-four days to implement. If you want to develop a habit of walking for ten minutes after breakfast, you might be able to implement it in as few as fifty days. The time and energy required to create better patterns varies, but regardless, almost always exceeds a month's time.[5]

So we must begin by preparing ourselves for the effort this task demands and committing ourselves to the long road required. Because as leaders, there is no shortcut. The environments in which we live and the people around us will often push us to develop patterns that can stall, sidetrack, or shipwreck us. You don't have to lead for long before you will be tempted to make poor decisions, to cut corners, or to follow the money rather than the mission. The decisions you make when you're faced with these temptations will determine which road you take and whether or not you'll develop the traits you need to succeed as a change maker. As *New York Times* bestselling author Ann Voskamp says, "do the next thing [even] when it's not the easiest thing."[6]

In discussing the formation of habits, we cannot ignore the shadow side of the conversation. The process of becoming a better leader is fraught with obstacles. As Nadia Goodman of *Entrepreneur* magazine points out, anticipating challenges is one of the keys to making sure habits stick.[7] Every temptation is an opportunity for transformation.

||||||||||||||||||||||||||||||||||||||||||||||||||||||||||||||||||||||||||||||||||||||||||||||||||||||||||||||||||||||||||||||||||||||||||||||

My sabbatical did me a world of good. I felt free. Free to discover what God had for me next. Free to start a new season in my life and work. Free to rebuild my leadership approach from scratch, this time with more insight into which leadership habits work and which don't.

At the tail end of that four-month sabbatical, I booted up my computer and opened a new document, just as I had when I first felt a stirring to take a break after that August lunch meeting with my friend Steve. I began thinking about the greatest leaders I've had the pleasure of knowing over the years and what they did that made them so great.

Then I thought about my own leadership journey and which habits most propelled me forward. As C. S. Lewis once said, "people need to be reminded more often than they need to be instructed." Typing furiously, I listed the most important habits under each of my mantra's three categories:

HUMBLE

- Self-Discovery: *Know who you are*
- Openness: *Share the real you with others*
- Meekness: *Remember it's not about you*
- Conviction: *Stick to your principles*
- Faith: *Prioritize your day so God is first*
- Assignment: *Live out your calling*

HUNGRY

- Ambition: *Develop an appetite for what's next*
- Curiosity: *Keep learning*
- Passion: *Love what you do*
- Innovation: *Stay current, creative, and engaged*
- Inspiration: *Nurture a vision for a better tomorrow*
- Bravery: *Take calculated risks*

HUSTLE

- Excellence: *Set standards that scare you*
- Stick-with-it-ness: *Take the long view*

- Execution: *Commit to completion*
- Team Building: *Create an environment that attracts and retains the best and brightest*
- Partnership: *Collaborate with colleagues and competitors*
- Margin: *Nurture healthier rhythms*
- Generosity: *Leave the world a better place*
- Succession: *Find power in passing the baton*

Twenty key habits reestablished for me my core leadership foundation. These are habits that provide the practical playbook for the next thirty years of my leadership journey. Ironically, these are habits that all great leaders have in common.

As I always told our interns, the characteristics of a Catalyst leader are vital. But so are their patterns. Better traits are the desired destination, but better habits are the road map. As a leader, you are responsible for putting these pieces into place and making them sustainable. Becoming a better leader personally doesn't happen on a whim. Or by accident. You have to work at it. You don't develop leaders by accident. You have to be intentional. Remember, leadership is hard work, and thus must be habitual work.

Since you're reading this, I suspect you're like the interns I sat down with every year. You may not be a recent college graduate who is willing to work for an hourly rate that borders on ridiculous, but you're eager to succeed. You're willing to learn and committed to doing whatever it takes to be a good steward of the calling you believe God has given you.

If that's you, consider the things I learned in a time of clarity and perspective. Then let's begin the process of change together. After all, becoming a better leader begins with building better habits.

Let the transformation begin.

HUMBLE:

WHO ARE YOU?

ONE

A HABIT OF SELF-DISCOVERY

KNOW WHO YOU ARE

The rumble of the airplane engine sounded like a freedom song. My sabbatical from Catalyst had officially begun. Next stop: London, England.

For the first time in over a decade, I had no workplace responsibilities, no e-mail in-box to clear, no deadlines to meet. As with any new endeavor, I began laying out my expectations for the sabbatical, and first on my list was self-understanding. The Brad who once was had already begun slipping through my fingers, and I needed to know who would stand in his place. I wanted to explore the depths of who Brad Lomenick *really* was when my professional identity had been stripped away. Freedom met fear as the plane prepared for takeoff.

London was to be more than a vacation. Steve Cockram—my old friend who had encouraged me to take this sabbatical in the first place—was waiting for me there. We planned to spend three days peeling back the layers of my inner onion and surveying what existed at my core. Could any seventy-two-hour goal be more ambitious?

Looking back, I was really setting out to accomplish this goal in reverse order. The time to develop a habit of self-discovery is not *after* one has spent a decade in leadership, but *before*. If one doesn't know who he is, how can he fully know how to live out what he feels called to? Influencers should lead from the inside out so that their identity shapes their leadership rather than the other way around.

For three days Steve and I walked along the famous River Thames and sipped on beer in English pubs and on great lattes in English coffee shops. We did a lot of wandering and nearly as much talking. We even visited a few landmarks, including the queen's second home at Windsor Castle, intermittently processing what this change of season meant.

Over a decade I had become Catalyst and Catalyst had become me. Every time Steve asked me personal questions about my identity, my primary impulse was to talk about Catalyst. Somewhere along the way, and I can't tell you exactly when it happened, I had erased the line between me and the organization I was leading. This represented a critical failure on my part to develop one of the essential habits that every leader should constantly cultivate: a habit of self-discovery.

Most leaders are mission-minded. They focus on goals and tasks and achievement. That's how they've ended up with influence to begin with. But the shadow side of this characteristic is the tendency to focus so tightly on a mission that one loses sight of the person pursuing it. Soon one becomes a ship without a captain, a body without a heart, a leader without an independent identity.

Unless one develops habits to combat this tendency, one's identity can slip further and further away over time. The more one works in a particular field, the more one becomes identified with the job and the reputation she has gained through doing it. Before long, one ceases to be.

But if an influencer has no identity—if she ceases to be—she creates a fragile reality. She conflates who she is with what she does and constructs a house of cards that depends on succeeding or at least maintaining some semblance of organizational cachet. That's why job loss obliterates so many leaders. The financial deficit stings, but the identity loss decimates them. They no longer have an answer to the question, "Who am I?" At least not one they believe.

Developing a habit of self-discovery means creating intentional rhythms whereby one observes who he is, listens to his life, and strives to define himself apart from his professional assignments. This habit helps a leader connect to an organization without being consumed by it. While it may not seem pragmatic, it is vital. Unless one is rooted in his identity, he can never become a change maker. For as Jean-Paul Sartre wrote, "to be at all you must be something in particular."

When it comes to identity, the danger isn't just that the leader will cease to be. It is also that she will unwittingly become someone she is not. From fashion to Facebook, unseen forces begin driving each of us to become something or someone that we think will propel us further toward our mission. Without even realizing it, leaders can become something they never intended. As Jay Z said on *Oprah's Master Class*, "knowing who you are is the foundation for being great."

Pastor Rick Warren has talked about this struggle and the way an ancient leader from a bygone era can inform modern influencers. After an Egyptian decree declared that Hebrew male infants should be put to death, baby Moses' Hebrew mother placed him in a small boat and sent him down the Nile River. Pharaoh's daughter discovered him and raised him as her own son.

At an early age, Moses had what Warren classifies "an identity crisis."[1] He was born a Hebrew and raised an Egyptian, born a slave and raised a noble.

Moses was tempted to forsake his Hebrew heritage and pretend to be Egyptian through and through. This would have certainly been a good career move. But God's providence and wisdom had made Moses a Hebrew. And the soon-to-be liberator couldn't forsake that. Even more, he couldn't ignore the Egyptians' unjust treatment of his countrymen and cousins.

But an often-missed verse about Moses—located in the New Testament rather than the Old, no less—teaches us something powerful about the importance of identity.

Hebrews 11:24 says, "By faith Moses, when he had grown up, refused to be known as the son of Pharaoh's daughter."

At first, one might assume this was as a brazen act of ingratitude. Pharaoh's daughter not only saved Moses' life; she made it better than he could have ever attained on his own. The level of education, nutrition, and experience he was given as Pharaoh's grandson were unparalleled in the world. How could he turn his back on a woman—the only mother he ever knew—who had given him so much?

> **🐦 YOUR SENSE OF IDENTITY WILL HELP DETERMINE YOUR SCALE OF INFLUENCE. IGNORE IT AT YOUR OWN PERIL.**

But when one considers the culture, the situation becomes clear. In ancient cultures such as this, one's ethnicity and nationality were a central building block of one's identity. So for Moses to live as Pharaoh's grandson would mean choosing a false identity in pursuit of greater influence. He decides instead to own his true identity, and as often happens, the decision leads to even greater influence.

Reflecting on this, Warren says, "Be yourself. Don't try to be somebody else. God made you for a purpose; he made you for a plan. There's nobody who can be you except *you*."[2]

Your sense of identity will help determine your scale of influence. Ignore it at your own peril.

Do you have the courage to be you rather than someone else? Are you brave enough to resist the forces trying to shape you into something you're not? If so, you're ready to develop a habit of self-discovery. Adam Braun, founder of the innovative nonprofit Pencils of Promise, tweeted, "[Your] self-discovery begins where your comfort zone ends."

Self-discovery is not one and done. There are no few silver bullets to utilize today so that tomorrow you'll have completed the process. Discovery, by definition, is a progressive reality. It is not something you've *done*, but something you should be *doing*. Discovery never ends.

Why?

Because human identities are deep caverns, and life doesn't grant humans enough years to reach the bottom.

> **SELF-DISCOVERY IS NOT A PRACTICE YOU COMPLETE, BUT A POSTURE YOU CULTIVATE.**

Various seasons—both the sweetest moments and the most devastating crises—will plunge you to new depths if you let them. I've learned attributes about myself at forty that I couldn't have at twenty, and vice versa.

To complicate matters, humans change over time. Once you feel you have discovered your identity, you've probably changed. So self-discovery is not a practice you complete, but a posture you cultivate.

I've found a few practices helpful in my own journey, but these require regular repetition as you form them into habits:

- **TAKE A TEST OR TWO.** Upon returning home from London, I took and retook several personality tests. I'd taken many of these before and pulled out my old ones to compare. It doesn't matter if you prefer StrengthsFinder, Myers–Briggs, DISC, or any other reputable test. Pick a couple and get started. Know very clearly your areas of strength. Take tests to understand your personality, and the *who* of who you are, looking for evidence and justification for why you operate as you do. You must first have an accurate understanding of who you are and where you are in life and a realistic picture of your current realities.

Once you have a few results in hand, review them next to each other and look for echoes. This gives you an emotionless snapshot of your identity, gifts, and passions. You don't get in the way of results. Instead, you can step outside of yourself and more clearly survey how you're built. Do this at least once every two years.

- **SCHEDULE REGULAR RETREATS**. You need to calendar at least one retreat per year. A couple is even better. These aren't professional retreats where you catch up on projects, or family retreats where you fill your time hanging with the kids at waterparks and playing miniature golf. These must be *personal* retreats where you focus on reflection and introspection.

  Go alone to a quiet place if possible. Make sure to unplug from your phone, e-mail, and social media as much as possible. (While I was on sabbatical, I changed my e-mail address. I found this unbelievably helpful.) Be intentional about answering specific questions about who you are and how you've changed since the last retreat. If your schedule allows, try to schedule one at least every eighteen months for a minimum of three days.

- **LEARN TO LIST**. I love lists, as those who follow my blog or have worked on my teams in the past can attest. From to-do lists to grocery lists to best practices, I feel as if I'm always compiling them. But one of the most important ones you can keep around is an identity list. Take time to list the central components that make you who you are. What do you prioritize? What energizes you? What grounds you in a sense of purpose?

  Survey the list after it is complete to see how many of the items you listed are tied to your job. This will help reveal if you're cultivating an independent identity. Keep this list in your desk drawer. Review and revise it every six months.

- **LEAD YOURSELF**. Self-leadership is a constant process. Self-leadership turns into self-awareness. Knowing who you are means leading yourself first. A leader's ultimate and most important role is to lead him- or herself. Great leadership starts with self-leadership, which means you know yourself. This is paramount. "Who am I?" is the foundation to "How do I . . . ?" Everyone wants to be great. But few are willing to put in the hard work to get there. You are your greatest coach. Start with you. This may be the most courageous decision you make. Courage is required to lead yourself first and make yourself better. You can't expect to pass on to your team what you don't have. The more I help *me* get better, the more I can help *we* get better.

- **BE MORE OF YOURSELF**. Stay true to who you are. Secure and self-aware leaders are confident and give confidence to others. In a shaky world a habit of self-discovery matters. Your identity is not what you do. It's who you are. And identity always comes before activity.

🐦 **IF YOU AREN'T INTENTIONAL ABOUT IDENTITY, YOU'LL IGNORE IT. AND *YOU* ARE TOO IMPORTANT TO OVERLOOK.**

Many practices can be a part of your habit of self-discovery. Feel free to borrow, modify, or replace my suggestions. But whatever you do, schedule identity-discovering exercises into the rhythms of your life. If you aren't intentional about identity, you'll ignore it. And *you* are too important to overlook. Nicky Gumbel, the vicar of Holy Trinity Brompton in London and founder of the Alpha Course, tweeted, "You can teach what you know, but you will reproduce what you are."

I remember the day vividly. On my third day in London, Steve took me to get a coffee at Costa Coffee, a well-known coffeehouse chain in the small town of Hedsor, west of Heathrow Airport about twenty-five minutes. We found a table outside, and I enjoyed a latte while Steve downed a stereotypical British tea. Getting to the coffee shop required a brisk walk of several miles to get to town from Hedsor Priory, where Steve's family lived in a beautiful, historic fourteen-bedroom house that looked out over the English countryside. Being there was like living in a Hollywood story.

We sat sipping coffee and tea, and I was feeling pretty good about the progress I'd made, when Steve dropped a bomb: "Brad, we're killing this person you've known. Today, 'Catalyst Brad' is going away.'"

I almost choked. The brazen suggestion frightened and even angered me. *How can I destroy the person I've been for ten years? And who does he think he is to even make such a recommendation?* Like every good coach, he gave me silence and space to process, and I soon recognized he was right. The words started to sink in.

It's not a stretch to say that "killing Catalyst Brad" was one of the most difficult tasks I've ever done. So far, we had worked on my personal leadership ability and forcing me to rest. That wasn't hard. But this was painful. It meant a chapter of my life was done ... over ... finis ... kaput. I was having to force myself to move on, to give up the false identity I'd crafted.

"Catalyst Brad" was barely "Brad" at all. I had stopped cultivating a habit of self-discovery, and it was time to begin again. My anger died down and I rested in knowing how necessary the task was. The facade I had created needed to die so I could locate the person beneath and help him live.

On the flight home I recommitted myself to being "Brad." No adjectives, no caveats, no prefixes or suffixes. Just "Brad." Pure and simple. Not about what I'm doing, but who I am and who I'm becoming. I repeated this refrain multiple times in the months following this trip: "Who you are is not what you do. What you do is not who you are. Identity is unchanging. Being comes before doing. *Who* you are determines *what* you do."

Decades ago, American poet Reynolds Price contracted a rare form of cancer that rendered his legs useless. When you cannot use your legs, everything changes. You can't just run to the mailbox anymore. Using the bathroom suddenly becomes a burden. When you decide to get off the couch and grab a swig of water, it requires serious effort. But the aspect of the experience that jarred Price the most was the resistance of his friends.

"When we undergo huge traumas in middle life," Price said, "everybody is in league with us to deny that the old life is ended. Everybody is trying to patch us up and get us back to who we were, when in fact what we need to be told is, 'You're dead. Who are you going to be tomorrow?'"[3]

I needed to return to my true identity and what is core about me, finding joy once again in the journey. Somewhere over the

Atlantic Ocean, I embraced the fact that the person I had created was dead. Now I needed to realize who I was going to be tomorrow and the next day and the next. Developing habits that help do this is difficult, but they are some of the most foundational in any leader's life.

3 TIPS ON SELF-DISCOVERY FROM DAVE LOMAS

DAVE LOMAS IS PASTOR OF REALITY SAN FRANCISCO AND
AUTHOR OF *THE TRUEST THING ABOUT YOU*.

We must remember that we don't find our identity; we receive our identity
from God. We are made in God's image and likeness. I utilize at least
three practices to remind me of this:

- **SABBATHING**: I practice this every week to remind me that my identity is
  not about how well I pastor or teach but about being a child of God. This
  is not a daily practice but it's vitally important for my daily life as a leader
  to remember that before I'm a leader, I'm a beloved child.
- **JOURNALING**: I spend time reflecting on my encounters and
  interactions in a journal I keep on my desk. Every morning, I try to
  jot some reflections down in a stream-of-consciousness style to
  open myself up to God and hear what God wants to say to me.
- **CONNECTING**: Being in honest community is vital. I live in life
  rhythm with three other leaders who know me completely and
  can both encourage me and call things out in my life that are
  inconsistent with my desire to be a godly leader.

PETE WILSON ON SELF-DISCOVERY

PETE WILSON IS PASTOR OF CROSS POINT CHURCH IN
NASHVILLE AND AUTHOR OF *LET HOPE IN* AND *PLAN B*.

Becoming authentic takes a great deal of self-reflection (getting to know
oneself), the courage to do the right thing, and a degree of selflessness. My
greatest enemy in becoming a true leader has been my desire to "be loved"
by everyone, leading to some unhealthy extremes in my life. Knowing this,
I must daily ask, "Am I making this decision out of a desire to 'be loved' or
to 'be loving'?"

Increase your self-awareness. I am blown away by just how possible (and likely) it is that we all have major blind spots in our leadership. We wonder why others make some of the choices they make. It's easy to see it in others, but difficult to see in ourselves. So how do we increase self-awareness? Slow down! Awareness increases as speed decreases. Most of us use the speed of life to medicate ourselves and ignore the major issues we're facing internally.

Know your own strengths, limitations, and values. Have relational transparency and genuineness. This involves being honest and straight-forward, and not playing games or having a hidden agenda. Be fair-minded and do the right thing. Effective leaders solicit opposing viewpoints and consider all options before choosing a course of action. They're open to the fact that they "may be wrong" and someone else may have the best idea. A true leader has an ethical core and knows the right thing to do.

TWO

A HABIT OF OPENNESS

SHARE THE REAL YOU WITH OTHERS

Many people don't know I grew up in a trailer park. I'm not ashamed of my upbringing, mind you; it just rarely arises in conversation. I first realized the effect my upbringing had on my current disposition while in London. Steve and I spent much time discussing my childhood and the way I developed a fierce sense of ambition. Growing up in a lower socioeconomic community meant I sometimes felt that I was "less than." I wanted to prove I was good enough and smart enough and capable enough to compete with others.

When I was in the twelfth grade, I won the Milky Way scholar athlete award. In case you were wondering, this is not given to the student who can eat the most Milky Way candy bars (though I am sure I would have won that too), but rather, for outstanding academic performance by student athletes. I remember a deep sense of pride when receiving the award in front of my classmates. I got the same feeling when I was named high school valedictorian and a top-ten senior at the University of Oklahoma.

In these moments I finally felt like enough. Even now, when I sense unbridled ambition welling up inside, I can trace the impulse back to childhood. My desire to achieve and succeed at all costs comes out of growing up in many ways wanting to prove myself and give evidence that I belong.

I've also realized that growing up in a trailer park made me a private, even sometimes disconnected person who often shies away from sharing the real me with others. I have to force myself to open up and be vulnerable with those closest to me. Talking about myself often feels uncomfortable. When things get too personal, I can change the subject like a champ.

When I penned my first book, a writer friend of mine read an early copy of the manuscript and commented, "You're always the hero in this book. You need to be more honest about areas where you've failed." I hadn't realized it during the writing process, but she was right. My tendency was to create a facade of uninterrupted success and hold my cards close to my chest, though in reality, I had failed as much as the next person. I pushed through the discomfort and reworked the manuscript.

I'm not alone.

Leading a company that produced large events for a solid decade means I've spent a lot of time in green rooms with "important" people. They are often places where everyone talks about books they've written, companies they've launched, money they've raised, and awards they've received. They keep others at arm's length, and work hard to create the aura of success. (There are exceptions to the rule, of course, but the trend indicates that I'm not the only leader who struggles with openness.)

Leaders can easily forget that people follow them, in large part, because of who they are. So you should own it. Yet, the higher one climbs the ladder of influence and power, the more difficult it is to be open. Ladder climbing typically leads to power tripping, which leads to a loss of influence.

Openness is the natural next step to self-discovery. Once you know yourself, you must ask, "What am I going to do with what I have come to know?" The answer is to move from a posture of self-awareness to self-disclosure.

A sabbatical forced me to get real: I was not as good a leader as I thought I was. I was stale, stressed, strained, and drained. And my failure to remain healthy was hurting those closest to me.

Kevin Kruse, a *Forbes* columnist and author of *Employee Engagement 2.0*, says that in order to be authentic, leaders must become "self-actualized individuals who are aware of their strengths, their limitations, and their emotions. They also show their real selves to their followers. They do not act one way in private and another in public; they don't hide their mistakes or weaknesses out of fear of looking weak... They are not afraid to show their emotions, their vulnerability and to connect with their employees."[1]

> **PEOPLE WOULD RATHER FOLLOW A LEADER WHO IS ALWAYS REAL VERSUS A LEADER WHO IS ALWAYS RIGHT. DON'T TRY TO BE A PERFECT LEADER, JUST WORK ON BEING AN AUTHENTIC ONE.**

Your realness will attract the next generation way more than your relevancy. People would rather follow a leader who is always real versus a leader who is always right. Don't try to be a perfect leader, just work on being an authentic one.

Like most habits in a leader's life, this is easier said than implemented. In the last couple of years, I have begun working to nurture it in my life. I found that several practices were especially helpful to me and are shared by many influencers I respect. I suggest that you do these too.

- **PERFORM AN ISOLATION EVALUATION.** Every leader runs the risk of quarantining himself or herself in an ivory tower.

Evaluate your own level of isolation by surveying the number and quality of relational connections in your life. Ask those close to you, "Do you think I am connected or isolated?" Lone Ranger leaders are destined for trouble. Even the actual cowboy character had Tonto.

- **DECIDE TO MAKE DEEPER CONNECTIONS.** Achieving depth in one's relationships is something that springs from a choice. It is a bit like deciding to ride a roller coaster even though one is afraid of heights. The cost is counted, the decision is made, and each subsequent choice becomes easier than the last. Challenge yourself to disclose personal information about yourself or ask serious questions during conversations with others. Relational depth often emerges from intentional dialogue.

- **ANSWER THE DREADED QUESTIONS.** Skilled leaders are often skilled communicators, and skilled communicators know how to dodge a question. But part of sharing the real you is just allowing the real you to be known, and this comes through responding to honest inquiries from others around you. Don't resist when people try to pry open the lid on your life's box. When someone asks a dreaded question you'd rather not answer, don't give in to the temptation to avoid it. Pause before responding, and if you can trust the person with the information, share honestly.

- **INVEST HEAVILY IN LONG-TERM FRIENDSHIPS.** Influencers, particularly extroverts and connectors, are always making new "friends." The tendency can be to invest up to a point in a set of individuals and then move on. You naturally share less of yourself with new friends. So leaders can end up answering the same questions and telling the same stories over and over without penetrating the surface of who they are. Is your closest friend group in a constant state of turnover? If so, you probably need to work on your level of personal openness.

- **LEARN TO SAY, "SORRY."** Often we become most real when we become most remorseful. Take time to apologize to those you've wronged or hurt. Set a day on your calendar each month when you send handwritten cards or e-mails to all the people you were a jerk to or need to offer an olive branch. You'll find that apologies can become soil where self-disclosure grows most easily.

- **FIND A CONFIDANT.** Every leader I know needs a confidant. Not someone on your team who reports to you or is a peer, or even your boss. Choose someone you can rely on, share with, lean into for tough decisions, and receive counsel from, as a trusted adviser.

> **🐦 LONE RANGER LEADERS ARE DESTINED FOR TROUBLE. EVEN THE ACTUAL COWBOY CHARACTER HAD TONTO.**

- **ESTABLISH A HABIT OF CONFESSION,** one of vulnerability and transparency, not concealing. A habit of confession brings things into the light. Confession leads to mercy and healing. As the leader, you must go first in terms of confession and authenticity. Authenticity flows from the top down, not the bottom up.

Authentic leaders must have the strength to admit when they've made a mistake and take the steps to fix it.

You don't expect a habit of openness from a pizza company, but Domino's has shaken up the industry. They told the world that their pizza sucked through a campaign called "Oh Yes We Did." To formally make amends and launch a new recipe for their signature product, Domino's had to admit the poor quality of their old recipe. The company realigned the perception of their product by getting real and embracing an openness and authenticity uncommon in the food industry. No other national brand in recent memory has led a new marketing effort with "We stink."

Facing their critics, the company worked to reestablish their pizza from the crust up. The pizza improved. And this is important: no matter how authentic and open, if Domino's had promised to get better and didn't, they would have lost all trust with the customer. But the new pizza was good, and lived up to the authentic brand promise.

Domino's CEO, Patrick Doyle, took to the radio waves and TV screens and made himself available for interviews and conversations. The company's profits soared 16 percent in the third quarter of 2014, and as Jesse Solomon of CNNMoney mentioned on Business Insider recently, "The pizza is actually better now, and the marketing campaigns are cheesy good instead of just cheesy." Shares of Domino's stock rose 30 percent from 2013 to 2014. Domino's moved into the slot of the world's hottest pizza chain.[2]

Leaders must make honesty and trust the standard for their organizational culture. In your organization, it starts with you. You have to lead on this. It's about the people believing the leader, and the leader always believing in the people. The more influence you gain and the more you have to lose, the less likely you are to be vulnerable and share your own struggles. We impress people through our strengths, but we truly connect with people through our weaknesses and areas of struggle.

Authenticity is built on trust. Trust is the prism through which all business and organizational transactions must pass. Unfortunately, in today's leadership culture, trust has completely eroded. Eighty-one percent of companies are not trusted.[3] The number is even lower for politicians. Let your yes be yes, and your no be no. And remember, "I don't know" is an okay answer. You aren't a leader because you know everything but because you know how to find answers and solve issues. Trust requires accountability and transparency. John Maxwell has noted, "Leadership functions on the basis of trust. When trust is gone, the leader soon will be."[4]

Believe it or not, learning to share the real you with others will make your family, friends, and staff stronger and more authentic too. There's a feedback mechanism that comes with openness: If you don't share the real *you*, others won't share the real *them*. In most settings, people are only as open as the person sitting across the table from them.

🐦 RELATIONAL DEPTH OFTEN EMERGES FROM INTENTIONAL DIALOGUE.

Additionally, the ability to share one's real self with others can set apart leaders from the pack. No one else is as much *you* as you are. Rather than covering up our worst parts and exaggerating our best parts, we should allow the unique mix of both to make us distinct and give us personality. Be the varsity version of you, not the junior varsity version of someone else.

Be 100 percent you and own it! Too many of us are trying to be the *next* someone, but instead, how about being the new and true you? Don't work on being the next Andy Stanley, Jim Collins, Oprah, John Maxwell, or Brad Lomenick . . . We can't take another one of those! Just be *you*!

As psychotherapist and leadership consultant Jane Shure points out, "If we buy into the notion that we are supposed to be like someone else, different from how we are, we are headed for trouble. We are not the same, nor should we be. Each of us has grown up with a distinct genetic inheritance, family patterns and school communities that have left indelible marks on us and within us."[5]

Embrace who you are, and even as you work to refine and improve that person, learn to share yourself with those around you. A habit of openness will help you feel freer and lead more effectively.

MIKE FOSTER ON OPENNESS

MIKE FOSTER IS COFOUNDER OF PEOPLE OF THE SECOND CHANCE.

In a leadership setting, I always try to lead with a story of how flawed I am, not how awesome I am. This can make leaders nervous because there are certain expectations others have of you. But authenticity puts your team at ease and helps them to understand that this is a place they can discuss what needs to be discussed.

If this makes you uncomfortable, start sharing some of these not-so-perfect things with your closest friends and family. Go to safe people. Slowly, make being open with others a part of your life.

But then there's the question about what to disclose and not disclose. Some things are nobody's business but yours. Parts of your story should be reserved for you and your spouse and your closest friends. You should always be able to disclose everything about you to at least one person, but as the circle expands, you should share less.

So vomiting all your junk on your team is selfish, not authentic. Don't force a therapy session on your team. Authenticity and openness doesn't just mean sharing; it means trying to connect better with someone else. It means stepping out and letting truth be the core piece of your life.

FOUR TIPS ON VULNERABILITY FROM BRENÉ BROWN

BRENÉ BROWN IS A RESEARCH PROFESSOR AT THE UNIVERSITY OF HOUSTON WHOSE INTERESTS INCLUDE VULNERABILITY, COURAGE, AND SHAME.

BRAD: If someone said they wanted to be more vulnerable in their life and leadership, what would you tell them to do?

BRENÉ: At least these four things . . .

- **START ASKING TOUGH QUESTIONS**. How and when do you armor up and why? How do you deal with uncertainty? Where do you really want to show up and be seen as a leader? What's getting in your way?
- **CHOOSE COURAGE OVER COMFORT**. Leaders have to be bold and open when it comes to uncomfortable conversations. There is no courage without vulnerability.
- **STOP, TEACH, AND MENTOR**. We're all so busy, but learn to do this. I'm working on this one constantly.
- **BE WILLING TO FAIL**. True courage is being willing to share all of our heart and all of our story. Vulnerability is the birthplace of courage, innovation, creativity, and change. Most of us are scared to death of being vulnerable. There is no innovation or creativity without failure. Period.

A HABIT OF MEEKNESS

REMEMBER IT'S NOT ABOUT YOU

Before I started my sabbatical, I dreaded the sound of a ringing phone. But during my sabbatical, part of me craved it.

When the opening bell of my sabbatical rang, I didn't expect to get nonstop e-mails. I didn't think the organization would dismiss the team, cease operations, and file for Chapter 7. But it is still a stark realization when the phone doesn't ring and everything keeps rolling without you. Sure, there was some transition—there always is—but checks were still cut and events were still planned and executed.

I was reminded in this moment of a philosophy I'd preached for years: *It's not about you.*

From staff meetings to e-mails, I'd used this phrase to hopefully instill a spirit of humility and cooperation among my team. I hoped it would remind us all that the organization's mission should always be more important than any individual's personal ambition. But the phrase is easier to say than it is to embody.

Leaders talk a lot about delegating and raising up protégés and "working yourself out of a job" and creating a culture where nothing would change if you suddenly resigned. But if you hooked those same leaders up to a polygraph machine while they talked about these things, the needle would be jumping. Everyone wants to be needed. We want to know that if we vanished tomorrow, our absence would be felt and our presence would be missed.

> **THE ORGANIZATION'S MISSION SHOULD ALWAYS BE MORE IMPORTANT THAN ANY INDIVIDUAL'S PERSONAL AMBITION.**

Many leaders will tell you they don't believe the universe—or even their department—revolves around them. But if you pop the organization's hood, you'll see a different picture. The team may not feel free to challenge the leader's opinion. The company's procedures may require the leader's approval or signature before even minor decisions can be finalized. Or the culture requires constant praise and approval of the leader.

Humility looks good on everyone. So if you want to know if your culture is too centered and dependent upon you, then ask these helpful diagnostic questions:

- Are others required to consult you before making basic decisions?
- Do you find yourself using the word *I* excessively?
- Must others keep you in the loop about details that do not directly affect your job?
- Do you have many trusted advisers who have permission to critique your decisions?
- Do you require regular applause and affirmation?
- Are people afraid to risk due to fear of backlash from you?
- Do you resist sharing blame if something goes awry?
- Do you receive criticism as regularly as you offer it to others?

Depending on how you've answered these questions, you may be realizing you've (perhaps unexpectedly) built a you-centric organization. If so, you need to get serious about developing a habit of meekness in your life.

iiiiiiiiiiiiiiiiiiiiiiiiiiiiiiiiiiiiiiiiiiiiiiiiiiiiiiiiiiiiiiiiiiiiiiiiiiiiiiiiiiiiiiiiiiiiiiiiiiiiiiiiiiiiiiiiiiiiiiiiiiiiiiiiiiiiiiiiiiiiiiiiiiiiiiiiiiii

One of the most influential leaders who ever lived is Jesus Christ. Two billion people on planet Earth today claim to follow his teachings. In his famous Sermon on the Mount, Jesus gave advice on how to influence others the way he did. His principles were as counterintuitive then as they are now, but one is especially relevant to this discussion:

"Blessed are the meek." (Matthew 5:5)

Jesus' advice in this simple statement runs against the leadership mantras most of us live by:

"Blessed are the strong."
"Blessed are the powerful."
"Blessed are the heavy-handed."
"Blessed are the connected."
"Blessed are the charismatic."
"Blessed are the promoted."
"Blessed are the in-charge."

Jesus knew what *Forbes* writer George Bradt has noted: "One of the most fundamental lessons of leadership is that if you're a leader, it's not about you. It's about the people following you. The best leaders devote almost all of their energy to inspiring and enabling others. Taking care of them is a big part of this."[1]

A habit of meekness is the counterbalance to the habits of

self-discovery and openness. As we focus on knowing and sharing ourselves with others, we must guard against turning inward and becoming exclusively selfish leaders. Developing a habit of meekness alongside these helps us know, share, and stay true to ourselves while remaining focused on others.

Meekness is not weakness. It's power under control. It's ambition grounded with humility and lived out in confidence, not arrogance. Quiet and appropriate confidence is way more attractive than loud and outspoken arrogance. Those who know the most many times are the ones who say the least. Humble leaders are willing to pass on the credit but absorb the criticism, push others higher while making themselves lower, and put the team's desires ahead of their own. A leader's job is to shepherd, not necessarily to always shine. It's about the mission, the team, and the tribe, not about you and your ego. Leaders today should be more conductors than solo artists.

> 🐦 **A HABIT OF MEEKNESS IS THE COUNTERBALANCE TO THE HABITS OF SELF-DISCOVERY AND OPENNESS.**

Humble leadership looks like my friend Nicky Gumbel, the vicar of Holy Trinity Brompton church, founder of the Alpha Course, and a well-known Christian in the UK. The first time I met Nicky, he was alone outside the backstage entrance of the Royal Albert Hall, one of the most iconic concert venues in all of London. He was unlocking his bike tied up to a streetlight, putting on his helmet, and preparing to ride home from a day at a conference, that he founded, of six thousand attendees. No entourage, no fanfare, just readying himself to ride a bike home. This image of the leader of a global church movement, standing by himself and unlocking his bicycle lock, has endured in my memory. It is a reminder of what meekness and humility really look like.

If you want to lead like that, here are a few tips to get you started:

- **CREATE A SYSTEM WHERE YOU AREN'T THE ONLY ONE PUSH-ING THE BUTTON.** Many organizations are set up such that all decisions funnel through a single person. Work to reorder your system to increase accountability and distribute responsibility.

- **START A "BETTER THAN I DO" LIST.** Leaders need to be reminded often that they aren't the only ones who are good at what they do. Keep a running list of people who do what you do *better* than you do. Whenever you find yourself reading too many of your own press clippings, spend some time reviewing this list to regain perspective. This has the added benefit of giving you a contact list where you can find people to learn from.

- **BEWARE OF THE "PARADOX OF THE PLATFORM."** Brian Houston says the platform, the stage, the bright lights, the accolades will destroy you if you haven't properly built a foundation on the realization that it's not about you. The platform should be for service, not for stardom. Never act as if you've arrived. New York Giants head football coach Tom Coughlin reminds his players, "[Be] humble enough to prepare, [and] confident enough to perform."[2]

- **INVEST IN THOSE WHO CAN'T RETURN THE FAVOR.** Leaders often invest the bulk of their energy in those who can pay them back. Meekness demands the opposite.

- **REWARD THOSE WHO PUSH BACK.** Healthy organizations incentivize moderate levels of dissent. Reward those who push back to help cultivate a diversity of opinions other than your own.

- **PASS ALONG POWER.** Power is one of the great corruptors of leaders. Power with purpose is incredibly appealing and a world changer. But without purpose, it leads to seeking popularity and greater platforms. We all deny our struggle with power in public, but realize its intoxicating pull over us in private. In the third temptation that Jesus faced in the desert, Satan said to Jesus, "I will give you all the kingdoms of this world in their splendor" (Matthew 4:9, paraphrased).

- **REMEMBER IT'S NOT ABOUT YOU.** Humble leaders make it about others, and always stay approachable. I meet people all the time at Catalyst events and leaders around the world who listen to the Catalyst podcast and feel as though we are friends, but we've never met. My goal is always to stay approachable and vulnerable and to realize it's not about me. I'm never as good as I think I am. I think people appreciate that you're like them, and feel that they are friends with you.

Looking back on my time with Catalyst, I wish I had worked harder to nurture a habit of meekness. It certainly would have prepared me for what I experienced during my sabbatical. Of course, my sabbatical wasn't the first time I realized I wasn't as important as I might have otherwise assumed. When I wrote my first book, I felt pretty accomplished. Something about holding a book in one's hand and seeing one's name has the power to puff up.

The first big event where I had a chance to sign books was at Catalyst in October in Atlanta. Next to the table where I was signing books, noted speaker, author, and founder of Going Beyond Ministries Priscilla Shirer was signing hers. People love Priscilla, and she has a massive following. Not surprisingly, her line wrapped around the building, and mine was only three people long (two people if you don't count my mother).

Pastor and author Jud Wilhite had a similar experience at Catalyst. After speaking at our event, Jud walked outside to his book signing table. Next to him was Hillsong's Joel Houston. Only a handful of people stood in Jud's line, while the end of Joel's trailed off in the distance. Afterwards, Jud came backstage and—as a good pastor always does—found a lesson in the experience: "That's God reminding me that it's not about me."

Those reminders were good for both Jud and me. They are good for all of us. As Hillsong Church pastor Brian Houston tweeted, "Pride refuses to be taught. Humility refuses not to be."

Leadership should never be about building a solar system around a leader. The quicker you can establish a habit of meekness, the better off you'll be.

3 TIPS ON HUMILITY FROM SIMON SINEK

SIMON SINEK IS THE BESTSELLING AUTHOR OF *START WITH WHY*.

BRAD: If someone said they wanted to be more humble in their life and leadership, what would you tell them to do?
SIMON: There are a few things . . .

- **BE THE LAST TO SPEAK.** When we are leading a meeting or are the senior person in the room, it is tempting to tell others what we think and then open the floor to thoughts and ideas. By waiting to be the last speaker, we allow others to be heard and feel like their ideas matter.
- **FIND SOMETHING YOU LIKE.** I can be quick to judge an idea or find faults before I recognize the benefits. So I try hard to find something I like when someone offers a thought. It's not just being polite; it's a way of keeping an open mind and remembering I don't know everything.
- **GIVE SOMEONE ELSE A CHANCE.** Humility is about letting others have a shot, even if we think we have the right answer. So don't let them know what you're thinking and give them the chance to make decisions (and mistakes) without fear of repercussions.

KRISTIAN STANFILL ON MEEKNESS

KRISTIAN STANFILL IS WORSHIP PASTOR AT PASSION CITY CHURCH IN ATLANTA, AND RECORDING ARTIST WITH SIXSTEPS RECORDS.

One of the keys to meekness is worship. This may sound like a predictable answer coming from a worship pastor, but worshipping Jesus is the very best weapon we have to fight against pride. Worship lifts our eyes and reminds our souls of who God is and who we are not.

Worship is a reminder that I was made by God for God and saved by grace to be a part of His story of glory and redemption on earth. God doesn't need me, but God chooses to use me. I realize it's a small role, but I'm totally okay with that if it means I get to be a part of God's story. Bottom line: There is no way to look at Jesus and not have humility flood your life.

FOUR

A HABIT OF CONVICTION

STICK TO YOUR PRINCIPLES

Sometimes being the prettiest person in the room can get you into ugly situations.

That's what my friend Kalyn Hemphill learned in her career as a model and actress. She began working with the Page Parkes Agency in Houston at the tender age of fourteen, but her star power has risen to new heights in recent years. Kalyn was named the winning model for season six of the television smash hit *Project Runway* and the spinoff series *Models of the Runway*. She has modeled for top designers and has acted in live theater, commercials, television, and film.

This story may seem like a fairy tale to many girls who dream of a career like Kalyn's, but today's modeling and entertainment industries are difficult places for people of character. She tells of how there is pressure for her and other models—particularly females—to sexualize their appearance and even pose nude.

But Kalyn's principles have led her down a different path. She's opted for modesty in her campaigns and has spoken out about the need to elevate inner beauty rather than sexuality. Kalyn has committed herself to helping young girls navigate the challenges associated with modern womanhood—including self-esteem and body issues.

Kalyn says her style icon is Audrey Hepburn because she knew how to be beautiful and modest at the same time.[1] When asked for her best piece of advice, she says, "Never compromise what you know in your heart is right."[2] She lives by her convictions, which is why she's becoming such an influential change maker in her industry.

Kalyn has built her life and career on the foundation that roots all great leaders: conviction. She knows what she values and why she values it. She has a strong moral compass, and she keeps it in plain sight so as never to get lost in the woods.

The best leaders are people of integrity and principle who know the difference between principles and preferences. They are willing to stand up for the right things and stand against the wrong things. These leaders value their reputations, their consciences, and their values.

Your private life determines your public legacy. Your public platform, influence, and impact require internal faithfulness, quiet confidence, and consistent wisdom. The best leadership moments will probably be the ones that nobody sees. The night before, the meeting afterward, the follow-up phone call, the insignificant work on the front end, that is where the real leadership is built and tested and tried. Work on those moments. A strong leader builds a habit of conviction, knowing that the times when no one is watching are when true character is built.

> 🐦 **THE BEST LEADERS PROTECT AND TREASURE THEIR REPUTATIONS, THEIR CONSCIENCES, AND THEIR VALUES.**

A habit of conviction is essential to becoming a change maker, but it is also the one habit that, if ignored, will destroy a leader most quickly. Every person of influence will face a moment—or moments—when they will be tempted to compromise their integrity. If the leader chooses wrongly at this critical crossroad, it can tear him down in a whirlwind of fury.

How many stories have you heard of pastors who had affairs and destroyed their ministries? How many times has a businessperson ruined her career because she got greedy and embezzled money? How often has a star athlete crushed his own dreams by using illegal drugs?

A habit of conviction means doing what is right instead of doing what is easy. And the further you go and the higher you climb in your leadership journey, the harder this gets. Talent and ability may help you get to the top, but it takes character and integrity to stay there. The depth of your character will determine the vertical depth and horizontal reach of your influence. The further and faster your influence extends, the deeper your foundation of character and conviction must be. Public service requires private submission. Deep roots allow for further reach.

Build who you are *off* the stage and behind the stage and beside the stage way before you start thinking about getting *on* the stage.

Looking back at my career, I now realize I was one of the lucky ones. I never had many ethical safeguards in my previous roles, but somehow I managed never to have a major moral failure. If I had to do it all over again, I would have been more intentional about establishing safeguards for my team and me. Character is like oxygen—it is something we often don't think about until it is depleted. But one can no more afford to live without conviction than without oxygen.

Don't bank on being a lucky one. If you ignore this habit, you do so at your own peril.

> 🐦 **LACK OF CHARACTER IS A FAST-ACTING VENOM FOR WHICH THERE IS OFTEN NO ANTIDOTE. SAFEGUARD WITH DEEP CONVICTIONS.**

Which principles do you refuse to compromise?

This question seems too simple. Almost cliché. But when I ask many leaders this question, silence fills the room and their eyes turn upward. It is precisely *because* this question seems simple that it is so dangerous. Many leaders *assume* they know what their most closely held convictions are, a false assumption that keeps them from ever naming them.

The first step to developing a habit of conviction is to identify one's convictions. What do you stand for? Which hills will you die on? What is not for sale or up for discussion? Or maybe, what do you feel you need to hide? You may want to create two lists: one of corporate convictions and one of personal principles. There will be some overlap, but they will probably not be mirror images.

> 🐦 **MANY LEADERS *ASSUME* THEY KNOW WHAT THEIR MOST CLOSELY HELD CONVICTIONS ARE, A FALSE ASSUMPTION THAT KEEPS THEM FROM EVER NAMING THEM.**

Keep this list front and center. Draft these on a piece of paper that you post in your office or tape to your bathroom mirror, or save them in a document on your computer's desktop so they are always close by and not easily forgotten. Your reputation is not for sale. Protect it at all costs. It takes years to build but only seconds to lose.

Second, you need to review, review, review this list. Place the date in your calendar or set a reminder in your cell phone. Your core convictions should be reviewed at least once a quarter, but perhaps once a month or a week at first. Feel free to add new items to the list as they come to mind. If you've drafted a corporate convictions list, schedule time at the end of regular meetings to review these with your team.

Why am I so adamant about this process? Because convictions are important and because repetition and review cement them in place. As the great boxer Muhammad Ali once said, "It's the repetition of affirmations that leads to belief. And once that belief becomes a deep conviction, things begin to happen."

As you become aware of and live by your convictions, here are a few other points to keep in mind:

- **PAY ATTENTION TO THE GRAY AREAS.** These are often the portal to missteps. Think through how you handle gray areas before you encounter them. It's easier than navigating once you get into them. If you're the boss, consider establishing guidelines for your employees. How do you deal with your expense report? Business trips with coworkers? Reporting to the IRS?

- **TREAT EVERY ASSIGNMENT AS IF IT IS YOUR LEGACY.** We often compromise our principles when we feel that the project or task is insignificant. Do it with quality and conviction and principle. Do what is right, instead of settling for the easy. Right takes work.

- **IF YOU SAY YOU'LL DO IT, THEN DO IT.** Even if it costs you. The value of a promise has plummeted in modern society. Don't contribute to its devaluation. Be a man or woman of your word. Trust is the foundation and bond of credibility. A great reputation means nothing unless you execute and fulfill the latest promise to your customer.

- **TECHNOLOGY AND INTEGRITY ARE CONNECTED.** Work devices are often used as a method for compromising integrity. People cheat on their spouses using work phones or look at porn on work tablets and computers. Make sure to require certain software on company-owned devices and install it on your personal ones as well.

- **DON'T TRY TO PLEASE THE NAYSAYERS.** The old song is right: you can't please everyone. Remember that the worst wheel on the cart makes the most noise. But there are still three good wheels that are silent and forgotten. Don't be distracted by the naysayers when pushing for change.

- **MAKE SURE YOUR CHARACTER OUTDISTANCES YOUR COMPE-TENCY.** Character > Competency. Develop the foundation of your "who" that is drilled deep, and developed way early and long before it's ever truly needed or compromised. Our integrity, moral compass, discipline, and honesty must constantly be advanced. As international speaker, pastor, and founder of the A21 Campaign, Christine Caine tweeted, "the spotlight will kill you if you haven't spent time in the dark room."

There's one glaring final point to discuss when it comes to convictions: What do you do when you've compromised one? A big one? When everyone knows you've failed? What then?

Apart from apologizing and making amends, I'll offer one encouragement: remember it is never too late to recommit to your principles. Trust may be compromised and relationships may be damaged, but that doesn't mean that your convictions are now irrelevant.

Hannah Jones, Nike's vice president of innovation and sustainable business, is a model of what it looks like to come back from failure and embrace integrity. When she arrived on the scene at Nike, the company was hated by champions of transparency and sustainability. Activists cited unethical practices in Nike's factories as the chief example for how the company had steamrolled the weak to make themselves stronger.

Jones has fought hard over the years to reform not just Nike's image but also their practices. Today, Nike is a leading corporate donor to major charitable causes around the world and is working to obliterate unethical practices in their supply chain. They have become far more transparent, and in 2011 were awarded a top honor for sustainability reporting.[3]

As it turns out, even big ships with big failures can return from the abyss. Don't you think you can too?

A habit can be established anytime. Even after the habit has been forgotten, abandoned, or temporarily overlooked. So no matter where you are in your career or life, no matter what you've done or failed to do, work to establish a habit of conviction today. Otherwise, you may find yourself unprepared to face the ugliest situations life will undoubtedly throw at you.

> 🐦 **BUILD WHO YOU ARE *OFF* THE STAGE AND BEHIND THE STAGE AND BESIDE THE STAGE WAY BEFORE YOU START THINKING ABOUT GETTING *ON* THE STAGE.**

HENRY CLOUD ON CONVICTION

HENRY CLOUD IS A CLINICAL PSYCHOLOGIST AND BESTSELLING AUTHOR OF *INTEGRITY*.

One of the biggest misconceptions about character development is that it is driven totally by "choices." Ergo, sometimes we wrongly think that we can make the right choices, and thereby develop character. In reality, character is developed not only through choices, but mostly by experience. In fact, the Greek word for *character* means "experience." In light of that, our habits must be habits that drive true "integrity" of character, or "integration" or "wholeness" as the word *integrity* implies.

The "choice-based-only" model relies upon existing strength of will, instead of true capacity building, which comes from outside of us. It must be given and internalized from the outside for the internal growth to take place. That is why relationship is key to any character growth.

I think there are three areas where we must structure various habits to drive character-building experiences: relationship, information, and practicing what we are learning. To include all three areas, I try to have daily habits of

1) reading or listening to new growth information each day,
2) intentional relational connection with someone or someone(s) who help develop my character,
3) making sure that every day has some sort of practice that stretches me in whatever area I am trying to develop,
4) making a habit of seeking feedback and true criticism from others each day.

CHRISTINE CAINE ON CONVICTION

CHRISTINE CAINE IS A PASTOR, ACTIVIST, FOUNDER OF THE A21 CAMPAIGN, AND AUTHOR OF *UNSTOPPABLE: RUNNING THE RACE YOU WERE BORN TO WIN.*

To help someone develop character, I would give them seemingly insignificant, invisible, unacknowledged, unapplauded, unrecognized jobs so they learn that everything is important. It is by doing what nobody wants to do that you end up doing what everybody wants to do. I would teach them to thrive in anonymity and obscurity so they actually become a leader and not only act like a leader in the spotlight.

This is crucial. I have often said that it is better to be in anonymity and to be marked by God than be in the spotlight and be marketed by man. The character and light of Christ in you must be stronger than the spotlight upon you so that your gift will not kill you.

DAN ROCKWELL ON CONVICTION

DAN ROCKWELL IS AN AUTHOR, SPEAKER, AND BLOGGER AT THE UBER-POPULAR BLOG *LEADERSHIP FREAK.*

First, I lean in when I hear complaints or criticism, even though my first inclination is to explain or justify. Second, I remind myself to see greatness in others, even though my first inclination is to focus on how great I am. Third, I tell people what I really think when it would be safer to tell them what they want to hear. Arrogance wants me to protect my standing or image. Humility says that honesty is more important than being liked.

I spend about two hours a day in self-reflection and writing. In order to do this, I get up between 4 a.m. and 5 a.m. on most days. I also seek feedback from both individuals and groups that can powerfully change me. It's part of the practice of humility. This practice comes from saying, "I could be wrong," to myself.

I make sure I'm meeting with leaders I admire face-to-face. Spend time listening. Take at least an hour a week and just listen to others. Keep notes on what others say to you. Ask questions. Don't judge. Just listen. Listening is central to the development of humility. Arrogance speaks. Humility listens. Listen to your frustrations and anger. Frustration is a gift. Don't bury it. Journal about it and ask yourself what you are going to do about it.

FIVE

A HABIT OF FAITH

PRIORITIZE YOUR DAY SO GOD IS FIRST

Back when I worked at Lost Valley Ranch, a beautiful four-diamond working guest ranch in the mountains of Colorado, I encountered a spiritual discipline that not only improved my faith but actually made me a better leader. It's called the "hand illustration," and was popularized by the Navigators ministry. My mentor at the time and founder of Lost Valley Ranch, Bob Foster—known as "Big Bob" to the staff and guests—taught it to me.

Imagine a hand gripping a Bible (or an iPhone with a Bible app loaded onto it). Each finger represents a different behavior that can empower you to "get a grip" on what the Bible says and teaches. Here are the five fingers of this approach:

- **HEARING:** Encountering sound teaching through sermons, spiritual talks, or faith-based books provides insight into how others are encountering the Scriptures.
- **READING:** Daily engaging the Bible oneself offers firsthand knowledge of God's Word.

- **STUDYING:** Digging into and writing down what one is reading helps us organize and understand what the Bible is trying to teach us.
- **MEMORIZING:** Depositing what you're learning into your memory bank makes the knowledge available for later retrieval.
- **MEDITATION:** This is the thumb of the hand because it is used in conjunction with the other four fingers. By meditating on the truth we're encountering, we begin internalizing it and allowing it to transform us.

This method may seem rigid to some, especially in an age of freestyle spirituality. But it gave me the structure I needed to develop the daily spiritual practices I required. But even more than that, it taught me that a healthy spiritual life doesn't happen via osmosis. It requires intentionality and regularity.

During my time at Lost Valley, many times over pancakes and the best bacon you've ever tasted, Bob and I would recite verses, by memory, together. I committed several hundred Bible verses to memory. They have served me well in the years since. I carried my memory verse cards with me on horseback rides throughout the Pike National Forest. While riding my horse, Bandit, at ten thousand feet through the Rocky Mountains, with multiple guests in my command, I would recount Philippians 2:4, or Matthew 5:16, or Ephesians 2:8–9.

I first adopted the hand method as a way to develop the fruit of the Spirit (see Galatians 5:22–23) in my life, but I soon realized that it enhanced my leadership ability. What leader doesn't benefit from developing more self-control or patience? Is there a CEO or manager or parent alive who couldn't use an extra helping of kindness or love? I think not.

Leaders often assume to their own peril that spirituality/faith is a good but separate part of their lives. Faith is less like your arm and more like your heart. It is not supplementary to who we are but integral. As such, you should work to keep it in good health.

A habit of faith is essential to your journey as a leader. The part you can't leave home without. Ever go on a trip and forget the one essential thing you have to have when you arrive at the final destination? For those of us who travel by air, you know it's a passport, or at minimum, a driver's license. Before 9/11, when living in Fayetteville, Arkansas, I was able to talk my way through security and onto my flight at the Northwest Arkansas Regional Airport without either. That would never happen today! This was the late '90s and the airport was so small that the security agents just knew me and allowed me through security with no questions. But today, I wouldn't make it through security in Atlanta without proper ID. That one thing missing would derail my trip. And I believe in life a habit of faith is that one thing you can't afford to not have on the journey.

> **FAITH IS LESS LIKE YOUR ARM AND MORE LIKE YOUR HEART. IT IS NOT SUPPLEMENTARY TO WHO WE ARE BUT INTEGRAL.**

One of the illnesses that often afflicts leaders is myopia. We begin to think that the story we are living and writing is *the* story. We become laser focused on our own goals, accomplishments, and responsibilities. But a habit of faith takes the pressure off. It reminds you that there is a bigger story of which yours is only one part. It allows us to stop worrying about what others are saying *about* us and instead consider what God might be saying *to* us.

In this way a habit of faith helps us realize that the fabric of our lives is composed of what God has done for us, not just what we are doing for God. It focuses us on what God is doing in us, not just what we are doing in the world. It shifts our eyes to what God is accomplishing through us, not just what we are accomplishing on our own. As the late Brennan Manning, author of the beloved *The Ragamuffin Gospel*, so eloquently said: "Our religion never begins with what we do for God. It always starts with what God has done for us."[1]

> 🐦 **THE MORE ONE SUCCEEDS, THE BUSIER ONE GETS. AND THE BUSIER ONE GETS, THE HARDER IT IS TO NURTURE SPIRITUAL VITALITY.**

Many leaders I meet, consult with, and coach have never nurtured habits of spiritual discipline. The more one succeeds, the busier one gets. And the busier one gets, the harder it is to nurture spiritual vitality. But those who want to be change makers must stoke a hunger for God's Word, prayer, journaling, service, and a lifestyle (rather than a once-per-week act) of worship. To maximize their influence, leaders must develop a habit of placing God first, not last. Let's view Monday through Friday as holy as Sunday. See the boardroom cubicle, classroom, and studio as sacred space.

The hand illustration doesn't work for everyone, and it doesn't claim to be a one-size-fits-all silver bullet. Every person responds to certain practices better than others and has certain schedule constraints that make various disciplines optimal. Still, here are some ways to begin developing a habit of faith in your life:

- **EXPECT GOD TO SHOW UP.** A habit of faith isn't a couple of extra items on your to-do list. It is creating space for God to show up. But an important part is *expecting* that God will. Pray for God to walk into your life. Keep an open mind, heart, and eyes. Invite the heavens to open and rain down. Part of faith is trusting that something will happen right before your eyes. Don't just go through the motions. Expect God to use your work and craft to bring Him glory. Selling auto parts, making widgets, distributing pipes, being a mechanic, and manufacturing furniture can be equally important in the story God's telling through your life. Maybe yourself available to God. Don't be concerned with being famous, successful, or the hero. Be concerned with being available.

- **UNPLUG YOUR EARS.** Too many Christians in the Western world only talk to God. But remember God's encouragement in the Psalms: "Be still, and know that I am God" (46:10). Insert thirty minutes or more of quiet into your week during which you listen *for* and listen *to*. I like to sit on my porch, especially when it rains. It's just an eight-by-eight-foot screened-in concrete slab, but that is my sanctuary. Find that place for you and commit to unplugging your ears to hear God's voice once per week.
- **FIND YOUR CHAIR.** Pastor Bill Hybels talks about the chair he sits in to meet with God on a regular basis. Do you have a place where you regularly are connecting with God, studying Scripture, praying, and meditating? (Again, for me, it's my outside porch.) If you don't have one, find one.
- **KEEP FAITH PRACTICES FLEXIBLE.** Nothing is worse than when life-giving spiritual practices turn into drudgery. Just because this is a habit doesn't mean it should become another notch in the humdrum of your schedule. If it starts to get stale, switch it up. Figure out what evokes your spiritual fervor and lean into that. For me it is music. For others it may be reading. Others need to talk with a friend. Others need to journal. Most people never

consider how they are spiritually hardwired, but taking your personal proclivities into account is critical. Where and when do you feel free to be spiritually open and receptive? My friend and worship leader Brian Wurzell recommends developing an appetite for the contemplative life and practices. Mix it up.

- **LIVE A HOLISTIC FAITH.** Look for God everywhere. Live and embrace the constant moments of God-breathed connection. Whether in church, at work, on your knees, in your closet, or driving in Atlanta traffic, God moments are always and everywhere around us. A few years ago, on a forty-degree day in early December, I walked up to the starter building at the most famous golf course in the world, St. Andrews in Scotland. A sacred moment at the birthplace of golf. Chad Johnson and I literally talked our way onto the course. As stubborn Americans, we weren't about to let the opportunity slide by. I had to buy a new outfit, rent clubs, rent shoes, and pay the green fee. But walking down the first fairway was a spiritual experience, and worth every penny. Both Chad and I were sobbing like a couple of school girls as we took in the beauty of the moment.

- **CONNECT TO A COMMUNITY.** This is a sticky one for a lot of people, especially those in the "spiritual but not religious" crowd. But connecting to a church community is critical to nurturing a habit of faith. This is biblical, and helps remind us that God is doing something bigger in our communities than just answering our morning prayers. Those who aren't a part of a church can easily become inwardly focused and risk developing a selfish spirituality. This doesn't mean going to a brick-and-mortar building with a steeple (though it might). You might start a house church or join a nontraditional congregation.

Regardless, we all need to be a part of a regularly gathering group of sojourners who can encourage us as we grow in our spiritual walks together.

Keep in mind that a habit of faith is never ending. You'll never wake up and say, "I've officially conquered this whole 'following God' thing." Instead, you'll need to keep stretching, growing, and progressing until your time on earth is complete.

> **THOSE WHO AREN'T A PART OF A CHURCH CAN EASILY BECOME INWARDLY FOCUSED AND RISK DEVELOPING A SELFISH SPIRITUALITY.**

Spiritual growth takes time. Following God isn't automatically fast, easy, and successful. Many times it's slow, difficult, and costly. Waiting on God is an active thing, not passive. Obedience and discipline take work.

During my sabbatical, I realize that my leadership had grown stale because my walk with God had grown stale. I expected Catalyst— *"It's a Christian organization, after all"*—to provide spiritual nutrients for my life. Following Jesus had been reduced to coordinating events for Christian leaders.

I knew I needed to take my spirituality to the next level, and I felt God nudge me to begin really investing in Passion City Church. I sensed God was moving through that congregation, and my friends who were rooted there bore witness to God's work. As I witnessed this movement of God, I wanted to be connected to it.

In previous churches I had merely been an attender. I hadn't been sewn into the fabric of a faith community for years. I was consuming rather than contributing. But I knew God wanted me to get involved—to serve, give, commit, and invest in the vision of a local body. So I jumped in feet first.

The energy of community is electric. It is joyful, celebratory, hopeful, reverent. Suddenly, I was being pastored. I was being discipled. I was being developed. I felt a sense of community and started doing life with the people of Passion City Church.

A lot of people stay home and stream a service online, and I don't want to discourage that. If you're growing spiritually this way for a season, you'll get no judgment from me. It's certainly better than many alternatives. But there is something special, even beneficial, about showing up to a place with a particular people for a particular purpose. Community, connection, and conversation only happen when we actually experience life with others.

I could have stayed home and practiced the hand illustration by myself for the rest of my life, but God wanted me to move forward and go deeper in my faith. And I sense God wants the same for you, for us all. We've lost our focus on faith as a generation, but passion for God is critical to becoming a change maker.

Begin implementing some deeper disciplines into your life today and then ask yourself, "What would God have me do next as I nurture a habit of faith?" As you focus on your inner life, you'll find that your influence will likely expand too.

JENNI CATRON ON FAITH

JENNI CATRON IS AUTHOR OF *CLOUT: DISCOVER AND UNLEASH YOUR GOD-GIVEN INFLUENCE.*

To really know and understand our callings, we have to first know our Creator. Knowing God brings clarity to one's calling. The more time we spend with God, the more quickly and clearly we can discern God's voice, and as a result, the more obedient we can be when God guides us. So I would encourage people to spend an hour per week seeking God. Perhaps that's in prayer, Bible reading or journaling. Maybe it's sitting in silence or soaking up nature. I ask people, "Where do you most feel God's presence and hear God's voice?" Then I tell them to go spend their hour doing that.

FOUR TIPS ON A HABIT OF FAITH FROM CHAD VEACH

CHAD VEACH IS THE FOUNDING PASTOR OF ZOE CHURCH IN LA AND AUTHOR OF *GEORGIA ON MY MIND.*

The four ways I try to develop a habit of faith and further my walk with Jesus:

- **DAILY BIBLE READING.** See the Life Journal (http://www.lifejournal.cc/) for a plan and the SOAP analogy (http://soapstudy.com/) for method.
- **LIVING IN COMMUNITY.** Based on Acts 2:42.
- **TALKING WITH GOD IN PRAYER.** An ongoing conversation with God.
- **ACKNOWLEDGING GOD IN ALL I'M DOING.** Proverbs 3:5–6.

SIX

A HABIT OF ASSIGNMENT

LIVE OUT YOUR CALLING

As my sabbatical rolled on, it grew increasingly difficult and discomforting. I was relaxing—a good thing—but I was also being forced to keep cultivating my inner life. I'd been plumbing the depths of my identity, and now I knew I needed to take the next step: reevaluate my calling and wrestle with one of the great questions of each of our lives—*what I am supposed to do*?

This may seem like a strange exercise for a forty-year-old at my professional stage. But every leader—no matter how old or accomplished—should regularly reflect on his or her calling.

> 🐦 **EVERY LEADER, NO MATTER HOW OLD OR ACCOMPLISHED, SHOULD REGULARLY REFLECT ON HIS OR HER CALLING.**

Many people conflate calling with identity. They confuse who they are with what they are made to do. While the two are connected, they are not the same. Identity is who you are, but calling is how you express that. Calling is your purpose. It is your guiding light. It is the string that connects our dots and allows us to feel fulfilled. It is, according to one of the most widely accepted definitions, where your deepest passions and your greatest strengths intersect.

The problem with this definition is that it is *too* simple. Where does one even begin? Do you create a list of passions and a list of strengths, and if so, how do you find connections between the two?

At this point in my sabbatical, I dug through my files to recover every old personality- and strengths assessment I could locate. Reviewing these reminded me of my gifts and passions. They allowed me to listen to how I tick and sense my innate proclivities.

After taking personality assessments, you won't automatically find your calling. None of them will spit out a piece of paper with "Calling" printed across the top in Courier New. But you should sense greater clarity and feel as if you're moving closer.

After letting the results marinate, write down what you think your calling might be. Try it on like a new shirt. See how it feels and whether you're comfortable wearing it. After a few days, you'll know if you've gotten close or need to tweak it.

> 🐦 **LEADERS WHO'VE NEVER INVESTED IN A COMPREHENSIVE PERSONALITY EVALUATION ARE MISSING OUT BIG-TIME.**

During this process, I stumbled across my calling statement, written when I was only twenty-four: "My calling in life is to 'influence the influencers.'" Even at that age, I sensed that I was called to gather, connect, equip, and inspire leaders who are making a difference in the world. But now I was trying to live this out in a new context.

How does one remain true to one's calling in different seasons throughout the course of his or her life?

This is where our next habit emerges.

Tailspin. That's what many people go into when they get laid off or their company files for bankruptcy. Why? Because many people think their job *is* their calling. But deep down we know this isn't true; otherwise one would be unable to live his or her calling before entering the workforce or after retirement. It would only be relevant while one is employed. But a job is simply an assignment.

There is a marked difference between a calling and an assignment, and failing to recognize it is a one-way ticket to the frustration station.

As a reminder, calling is the intersection where your greatest strengths and deepest passions come together. Finding that sweet spot is paramount. But while your calling expresses how you were built and what you were designed to do best, an assignment is the way you live that out. Calling is made up of seasonal-purpose assignments. The sum of our seasonal-purpose assignments should add up to our greater calling. Assignments give evidence of calling and purpose through different seasons.

> 🐦 **THERE IS A MARKED DIFFERENCE BETWEEN A CALLING AND AN ASSIGNMENT, AND FAILING TO RECOGNIZE IT IS A ONE-WAY TICKET TO THE FRUSTRATION STATION.**

Though one's calling may change slightly over time, one's assignment will change many times throughout the course of one's life—both in vocation and personal life. The former is increasingly true for young leaders. Forty years ago, a person may have worked in a steel mill for forty-five years before taking a pension. But such tenure is almost unheard-of these days. According to the Bureau of Labor Statistics, the median number of years an American worker has been in his or her job is 4.4 years. This is drastically less than the 1970s and '80s. Men in the United States will have 11.4 jobs on average throughout the course of their lives; women have 10.7.[1] Each of these jobs marks a new assignment for living out the same calling.

I've had three major seasons of vocational assignments so far:

- *Lost Valley Ranch*: On paper it may have looked as if I was being paid to play cowboy. But as a ranch foreman, I was overseeing our clientele of business owners, ministry leaders, pastors, and entrepreneurs. I was "influencing influencers."
- *Life@Work* magazine: This publication's mission was to help bridge the gap of faith and work, and provide resources to organizational leaders. As chief development officer over this publication, I was living my calling to "influence influencers."
- *Catalyst*: I oversaw the largest movement and gathering organization of young Christian leaders in America. We produced several large events each year, and as president and lead visionary, I was working again to "influence influencers."

Right now, I'm in a fourth season as a leadership consultant and author. I sense this will probably not be a permanent assignment, but it is still fulfilling because it is connected to who I am and what I was designed to do best.

From the outside one might think I didn't know my calling. After all, I bounced from the hospitality industry to the publishing industry to event production to writing and consulting. But the common thread sewing together each of these assignments is calling, which is rooted in and connected back ultimately to who I am, through a purposeful calling statement.

IDENTITY	CALLING	ASSIGNMENT
Who you are	What you were designed to do best	Where you live out your calling
Does not change	Can change somewhat	Changes, probably many times
The drive	The direction	The destination

Don't feel that you have to be 100 percent ready for the next assignment. I've never been fully prepared for my next season. All three of my calling-assignment seasons I wasn't ready for, but jumped into each with the same level of confidence and expectation I had for the previous one. I stepped into the "unknown" assignment season because I was confident in my calling. The thirty-thousand-foot-level calling statement gives me confidence for stepping into the three-thousand-foot-level new season. I sense this is true not just for me, but for many of us.

Of course, assignment is not limited to the workplace. Your assignment may take place in the context of your church or a community organization or family. You may have a season of assignment as a stay-at-home dad or mom. And sometimes, you'll find yourself in the midst of a couple of assignments at the same time. You just need the proper perspective to see how it is all connected.

How do you cultivate a habit of finding the right assignments and determining when it is time to look for a new one?

Ah, good question. I'm glad you asked.

First, you need to regularly evaluate your satisfaction. I've heard a lot of people say, "I work to live rather than live to work." That sounds cute, but it's usually a rationalization tool for those who hate their jobs so they can muster the strength to endure them. The truth is that life is too short and too much of it is spent on outside entertainment activities to succumb to that kind of logic.

> **YOU SHOULD LOVE YOUR ASSIGNMENT, NOT JUST ENDURE IT.**

You should love your assignment, not just endure it. You can't expect every day to be glamorous and to fire you up. Some things you just have to weather. But if you dread getting out of bed and diving into your occupation or engaging with your assignment, something must change. You should love what you do. Or at least like it. Don't settle for just going through life enduring Monday through Friday.

To cultivate a habit of assignment, sit down semiannually and ask yourself critical questions about whether or not you are content in your current assignment:

- *Do I love what I do?*
- *Do I feel I'm just enduring this?*
- *Has this become a means to an end (money, fame, significance), or does it give me a sense of purpose?*
- *Is the greatest intent of my week to get to the weekend or next vacation day?*
- *If someone told me that I had to quit this assignment tomorrow, would I be relieved or disappointed?*
- *Am I still being challenged?*
- *Would my spouse or close friends say that this assignment is right for me?*
- *Is where I am integral to getting me where I really want to be?*
- *Am I dreaming about next phases more often than thinking about what's in front of me?*

After asking these questions, if it is clear you aren't satisfied, you have two choices: work to change the dynamics of your current assignment or begin looking for a new one. Stave off the guilt, and grant yourself permission to be honest and take action. It's too important.

A habit of assignment is about doing, not dreaming. It's about action, not ideas. It's not a right or wrong answer, but a better or best answer. Assignment gives fulfillment, connects the dots, and provides context and skin to our purpose. "Be who God meant you to be and you will set the world on fire," said Saint Catherine of Siena.

Back in my Lost Valley Ranch days, I managed the ranch dudes, oversaw the welfare of our animals (including almost 150 horses), and cared for the nearly one hundred guests who visited our property in a typical summer week. One of the most entertaining moments in my week occurred the first time the three came together.

When a new crop arrived to the ranch each Sunday, guests were assigned horses to ride for the week. This isn't as easy as drawing a number from a hat and tossing it into the crowd. You don't want a wild teenager who wants to gallop nonstop sitting on an animal riddled with arthritis who can barely trot. And you don't want to place a rookie atop a stubborn stallion who doesn't take orders from a rider without an extra dose of confidence. A horse's personality must match its rider, and pairing the two was usually a mixture of comedy and drama.

Guests were summoned to the corral, and one by one, they would be hoisted atop a block wooden horse with a saddle on it. Stepping back, I'd begin sizing them up. I'd take note of their posture and whether they were making stupid faces at their friends or siblings. Then, I'd ask them a handful of questions about their personality, desires, and riding experience. Each one would help me sort through who the best match for them was.

Calamity Jane, Buttercup, maybe Molasses? Certainly not Navajo Joe. He is an angel, and I wouldn't do that to him.

Finally, I'd shout out a horse's name. The guest's name would then be scribbled next to the animal's on a giant chalkboard. Once the name was spoken, the pair would unite and the matter was settled.

I've often thought about assignment a little bit like this. There is a process where one stands back and considers who he is, what he wants, how he acts, and what makes him spring to life. And then he considers what possible matches are out there that he might experiment on for a season.

On the ranch this may have been the single most important activity of the entire week. A good match meant everything else the guest did would be enhanced. A bad match could ruin an otherwise pleasurable experience. In the same way, nurturing a habit of assignment may determine whether you spend your life being constantly bucked or galloping off into the sunset.

Don't ever lose that sense of curiosity, wonder, and excitement for the calling on and in your life. Fan those flames. Be open to the voice of God directing you toward what's next.

SHAUNA NIEQUIST ON ASSIGNMENT

SHAUNA NIEQUIST IS AUTHOR OF NUMEROUS BOOKS, INCLUDING
BREAD AND WINE.

I've developed a habit of calling by practicing it. The biggest thing at play here is time. We must consider how we steward our time to make sure we give the most time to the things that are at the center of our calling. The hardest work is figuring out one's calling for a particular season, and the next difficult thing is to walk away from things that are fun and enjoyable but may not be at the center of one's calling. Stay accountable to the center circle in your life. A lot of that comes from saying it out loud. It's important to speak the center of your true calling.

Calling has through lines, but it does change season to season. It makes decision making easier when I look at things as existing for a time and season. If someone is considering committing to something for the next season, I suggest they ask five people who know them really well and know their life if they should. That's a great way to discern an opportunity and the next season of calling.

Calling is about identity and one's long-term makeup, but assignment is seasonal. Your calling informs your assignments, but they are different. My calling as a writer is not specific enough to give me marching orders for a season. So I need seasonal assignments with very specific marching orders.

As a result, I don't have five- or ten-year goals. I believe in what I'm called to do, and I have tied my goals to *this* season.

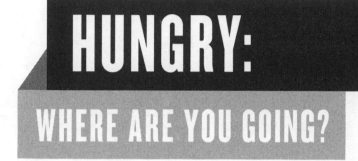

HUNGRY:

WHERE ARE YOU GOING?

SEVEN

A HABIT OF AMBITION

DEVELOP AN APPETITE FOR WHAT'S NEXT

One of my rules for leadership is "Beware your greatest strength." Why? Because often an influencer's unguarded greatest strength is also his or her greatest weakness—and therefore turns into his or her greatest temptation. Your best can bring you down.

One of my good friends, for example, runs a nonprofit. His confidence has allowed him to grow the nonprofit from a tiny dream to a full-fledged organization with a handful of full-time employees and a growing annual budget. He is able to walk into boardrooms and living rooms and ask for funding from millionaires and CEOs when others would shrink back and beat around the bush.

But his confidence also has a shadow side. Many people, upon meeting him, think he is egotistical. He can often come off as a know-it-all who is trying to steal every show he encounters and own every room he enters. My advice to him, as with so many others, is "Beware your greatest strength." His confidence is good, but it needs to be bridled if he wants to maximize its effectiveness.

My greatest strength, and coincidentally my greatest weakness, is ambition. It propels me forward, pushes me to set goals, and drives me to meet deadlines. I'm always looking for ways to improve, and I'm never going to settle for "good enough" or "high enough." But if left unchecked, my ambition can also cause me to run roughshod over team members and those I care about. By focusing on the horizon, I can become blinded to those right in front of me. Without check my ambition will leave people strewn in the ditches beside and behind me.

Once at a staff outing, I took my team to one of those places you go and play arcade games and collect tickets. Over an hour we had pooled together a bucketful of tickets. Individually, we might have cashed in for a bunch of pencils or bouncy balls. But my assistant, Michelle, had the idea to put our tickets together and purchase a set of two dolls—one was an angel and one was a devil. The dolls were the same, except wings poked out of one's shoulder blades and horns protruded from the other's head.

"We *have* to buy those dolls," Michelle said. "That's Brad and Darb."

"Darb" (Brad spelled backwards) is what my team had dubbed my alter ego. When my ambition ran wild, Brad's wings fell off and he sprouted horns. Darb yells a lot, and drives his team too hard. He still gets things done, but he will leave people in the ditch. Everyone hates Darb even though he is wildly productive. He focuses on procedures and productivity, rather than people. Brad is ambitious, but Darb is blinded by his ambition.

> 🐦 **DEVELOPING A *HEALTHY* HABIT OF AMBITION IS ONE OF THE MOST IMPORTANT TASKS OF EVERY LEADER.**

After that staff outing, Michelle would randomly place one of the dolls outside my office door depending on which person was in control that day.

Looking back, I wish I had worked harder to ensure that the Brad doll remained next to my door and the Darb doll stayed in the drawer, because developing a *healthy* habit of ambition is one of the most important tasks of every leader.

||||||||||||||||||||||||||||||||||||||||||||||||||||||||||||||||||||||||||||||||||||||||||||||||||||||||||||||||||||||||||||||||||||||||||||||||||||||||||||||||||

Ambition is one of those words that is often preceded by a negative adjective. We may talk about "bad ambition" like the greed of a CEO or a power-obsessed politician or a celebrity starving for greater fame. We may also speak of "blind ambition," like when Darb only sees the goal and not the people around him. For some the characteristic has become a dirty word—synonymous with being self-serving, dog-eat-dog, ladder-climbing, or self-promoting. But it doesn't have to be disastrous or destructive.

Never satisfied, but always content is the posture of a properly ambitious leader. Your posture of ambition should be one of the hungry second, not the arrogant first. Act as though you don't belong, but work as though you do. No one enjoys being around someone who thinks she deserves way more credit than she really does. Stay hungry and motivated, not arrogant and entitled.

> 🐦 **AMBITION IS BURIED DEEP WITHIN YOU. ONCE IT IS UNEARTHED, YOU MUST BRIDLE IT TO KEEP IT IN HEALTHY BALANCE.**

I think of ambition as I do money or technology—morally neutral but susceptible to manipulation. Gang leaders have ambition, sure. But so did Mother Teresa. Ambition isn't inherently evil, but leaders must learn to channel it.

Some people are born with an extra helping of it, and they run the risk of developing Darb-like horns. Others have to really work to nurture ambition in their lives and fight the temptation to become too comfortable wherever they find themselves. No matter which end of the spectrum you find yourself on, the characteristic is buried deep within you. Once it is unearthed, you must bridle it to keep it in healthy balance.

In its purest form ambition is a knowledge of and appetite for what's next.

I've always had quite a heavy dose of ambition. Always wanted to be the best. Always felt the pull to get better and challenge myself. To go after what's next. Whether it was the free throw shoot-out contest in elementary school or the spelling bee, I wanted to win first place. Whether it was being the fastest kid in elementary school (which I was, and held a record in the 100-yard dash), or racing good friend and radio host Ken Coleman on Thanksgiving Day a couple of years ago. Which didn't end well, as my aging legs both gave out and I violently popped both hamstrings about twenty-five yards into the race. I quickly realized my has-been status! My appetite for what's next had caught up with me. But a habit of ambition is much more than this.

The word *appetite* is critical and intentional. An appetite comes naturally, but it has to be fed correctly in order to yield health. Look at your own life and ask, "How am I feeding my ambition appetite?" and "Is it producing health in my life?"

When your ambition appetite is properly fed, it will yield a desire to achieve, to grow, to perform, and to do one's best. It will also yield a healthy job environment, healthy relationships, and a healthy work-life balance. If you don't feed your ambition appetite at all, you'll yield laziness, stagnancy, and ineptitude. If you feed it wrongly, you'll end up with broken relationships, high turnover, and a poor reputation.

A healthy appetite of ambition steered correctly can actually fuel other healthy habits, especially in times of transition. Ultimately, many habits emerge and end up sticking during times of change. This has been true in my own life. I've visited London multiple times in the last five years. My hotel of choice is in South Kensington, adjacent to Hyde Park, a historic and well known Central Park equivalent piece of property in central London. Now I've stayed close to Hyde Park in the past, but never felt inclined to run through the park. However, this year, in the midst of a change in lifestyle and losing over forty pounds, I was incredibly motivated to run through Hyde Park. The same is true with our leadership and particularly with our appetite of ambition. We can have the same routine, same schedule, meetings, staff, and goals, but until we change our perspective and our intentionality with what is put in front of us, we won't see change and impact occur.

Here are some tips to help you feed your ambition appetite well and nurture this critical habit within yourself and among your team:

- **SKETCH TOMORROW.** Stephen Covey, the late author of the iconic *The 7 Habits of Highly Effective People*, famously said that leaders must "begin with the end in mind."[1] But it's hard to believe what you can't see. If you're artistic, actually draw or paint an image of what your desired future looks like. If you're better with words, write it into a story. To create goals, you need to know where you are headed. But many people don't set goals because they have never dreamed specific dreams about the reality they hope to create.
- **SET GOOD GOALS.** Most people have some sort of goals, but many of their goals are not good ones. The best goals are specific, not general. They are attainable, not unrealistic. They are challenging, not easy. They are measurable, not undeterminable. And they are clearly communicated, not assumed. Make sure you have clear and specific goals for yourself and your team that can be evaluated after a set period of time.
- **STOP TO CELEBRATE.** Those who have no ambition won't recognize cause for celebration, and those with too much

ambition will move on to the next goal. Whenever you or one of your teammates accomplishes a major goal, pause for celebration. Celebrating a goal encourages goal-setting and achievement. This is a springboard to setting and pursuing new goals while nurturing healthy relationships.

- **CREATE COMPETITIONS.** One of the quickest ways to motivate ambition is allowing people to compete against each other with a reward system in place. Healthy competitions must be visible, kind, and constructive. Employers are often skilled at negative reinforcement—from reprimands to layoffs—but less able to craft compelling positive reinforcements. Of course, it's easier to berate someone when he or she messes up than to create visible and constructive competitions that spur people to greater heights. In competition, both parties usually go further than they otherwise would.

- **UNDERSTAND YOUR ROLE.** Simply put, the role of a leader is to hire the right people, put them in the right roles, give them the resources they need, and then get out of the way. Great leaders make everyone around them better. A habit of ambition is best lived out through others around you and through helping them fulfill their dreams and desires and callings.

- **BECOME AN EXPERT BEFORE YOU NEED TO.** Work as though you're in the position you want next. Practice as if you're the starter. Act, lead, dream, dress, create, and speak as you would in the role that is next for you. This is way more demanding. Demand perfection from yourself before anyone ever demands it of you at an organizational level. When I was a sophomore in high school football, my number got called in a playoff game against

Checotah, and I quickly realized I was facing an All American named Tracy Scroggins, who went on to play in the NFL for the Detroit Lions. He ran over me, and it was an eye-opening experience. Practice as if you're the starter! Work as if you're in the position you want next. That way when it's your turn to come off the bench on the sideline, you're ready. As Zig Ziglar once said, "Before a person can achieve the kind of life he wants, he must think, act, walk, talk, and conduct himself in all of his affairs as would the person he wishes to become."[2]

- **KEEP GOING AND KEEP TRYING.** Rejection is not the end of your influence. Experience creates expertise, so keep getting better. Great leaders continue to improve and don't allow for mediocrity to set in. Push yourself on a daily basis. Get up early, stay up late, and keep plugging away. Rejection is not the end of your influence, but may actually be the beginning of something great. A habit of ambition many times is built because of more nos than yeses. One of the greatest bands of all time, U2, was rejected in 1979 by a record label. Just because you get a no doesn't mean it's not supposed to happen. A no just means you are closer to a yes.

Ambitious leaders provide solutions, not just ideas. They constantly move toward completion. They honor others by showing up early and finishing on time. They always anticipate what needs to be done next and are always one step ahead, and they work on items they weren't asked or told to do but know have to get done. They move the needle wherever they are placed and are always looking for ways to improve the process. They are disciplined in their learning and understand the power of becoming an expert, no matter what level or role they play in an organization. Ambitious leaders write down everything immediately, knowing they will probably forget if they don't and that writing it down makes it a priority. They take initiative and remove things from leaders' plates around them.

Creating a culture of ambition—the healthy kind—will pay huge dividends for leaders. Ambition gives you and your people the will to do better, fly higher, accomplish more, push harder, and create something special. Nothing makes a leader more audacious.

Kevin Allen, author and accomplished entrepreneur, says it this way:

> Leadership starts with a special kind of quest: a real ambition. Numbers, facts, or figures do not motivate people. Rather, people are enchanted when they have the chance to create something extraordinary and when they can see clearly the opportunities they have to participate. Real ambition is the engine of any endeavor, it's the creation of something good that didn't exist before. Establish it, enlist for it, and fight for it and you'll achieve whatever you seek for yourself and for the people who will make it happen.[3]

Everyone is born with a measure of ambition, but the rest still must be nurtured. Ambition is important in every life phase. Talent built on a foundation of humility, continually fueled by hard work and a make-it-happen attitude, will succeed.

So whether you are currently climbing the corporate ladder, taking a break in midlife to reevaluate, or straining toward retirement, you need to develop an appetite for what's next.

After all, if you're not hungry, you're not healthy. And if you're not eating, you're not living.

SEVEN TIPS ON AMBITION FROM SCOTT DREW

SCOTT DREW IS THE HEAD BASKETBALL COACH AT BAYLOR UNIVERSITY.

I develop ambition and hunger as a daily habit in the following ways:

- Praying for God's direction for the day
- Organizing a list of things to accomplish
- Having a plan of action to complete these goals
- Surrounding myself with other ambitious and hungry individuals
- Having a drive and desire to outwork the competition
- Making sure my staff and players organize their days so they can maximize their productivity
- Being a servant. After all, Jesus came to serve and not be served.

FIVE TIPS ON AMBITION FROM TIM ELMORE

TIM ELMORE IS THE PRESIDENT OF GROWING LEADERS AND A BESTSELLING AUTHOR.

I have several layers of habits to stoke ambition.

- At our Growing Leaders office, we start our week with a stand-up meeting in which we write on a wall all of the "big rocks," or top goals, for that week. Because we are standing up, the meeting stays short, but it provides accountability to me and our team to follow through on the most important priorities.
- I meet on a regular basis with six mentors who push me to keep pursuing my personal mission and our organization's mission.
- I post the biggest projects for the year on the wall in front of where I sit and look at them daily. It's a list of fourteen items I plan to achieve by December 31.

- I have drafted a "life sentence," which is a statement summarizing the outcome I'm shooting for as a leader. I keep it in front of me at my home office. I see it every day.
- Healthy leadership is about "who" before "what." The moment I turn leadership into a series of behaviors, I'm in trouble. I can't divorce leadership from the heart. It is being before doing. The roots must be strong, the trunk must be stable, and the fruit must be real and naturally tasteful.

EIGHT

A HABIT OF CURIOSITY

KEEP LEARNING

The Hillsong bands have achieved success that many others only dream of. They've had many songs hit the *Billboard* charts. In 2014, they were nominated for ten GMA Dove Awards, including Artist of the Year and Song of the Year, and were the subject of a new documentary. Their powerful worship songs, such as "Mighty to Save," are belted out by hundreds of thousands in churches around the world each week. Their touch is Midas-like.

Given the level of success that Hillsong has enjoyed, I had some preconceptions about what they would be like. After all, I met more than my share of divas in my decade with Catalyst. But when I first encountered the members of Hillsong United at an event outside of Los Angeles, my assumptions could not have been more wrong.

The music at Catalyst events is always interspersed with first-rate speakers sharing groundbreaking and insightful content. Normally, when a band finishes a set, they go back to the green room behind the stage to relax, have a cup of coffee, and goof off a little bit before they have to go back out. They aren't typically engaged in the speakers. And who would blame them? These bands play dozens of conferences each year. They've heard much of this content before.

When I walked into the green room and encountered the Hillsong United band after their first set, I was nearly knocked off my feet. The band members were huddled together around a tiny television with a closed-loop feed of the first speakers. Then they watched the second presentation. Then, the third. Many of them had Moleskine pads, and were furiously scribbling notes. No one was talking. No one was checking text messages.

You could have knocked me over with a cough.

Observing Hillsong United band in that moment, I had uncovered one of the secrets to their success. They have never let fame go to their heads and have instead maintained a habit of curiosity. Rather than transition from the role of student to the role of teacher—as most accomplished people do—they remained pliable, always maturing and improving. Catalyst was not just another "gig" for them; it was an opportunity to learn.

As I witnessed this scene, I thought to myself: *This is a picture of true leadership.*

Most leaders follow a particular trajectory. The early stages of one's life and career are often marked by unbridled curiosity. The leader amasses college diplomas, graduate school degrees, and specialized certifications. She will often attend conferences and read books within her field and accept low-paying or unpaid internships just for the benefit of learning something. After some time, the leader's curiosity begins to pay off. People notice her effort and respect her industry knowledge. Promotions and raises follow, and soon she may be asked to present in meetings or speak at conferences herself. But as a leader's career surges, her curiosity often sinks. She has all the degrees

> 🐦 **AS A LEADER'S CAREER SURGES, HIS OR HER CURIOSITY OFTEN SINKS.**

she needs, and who can afford to take an internship at this stage of the game? Her busy schedule doesn't allow time to read much, and she wouldn't be caught dead sitting in a conference crowd after being onstage. If the leader's life were a movie, this is where it moves from feel-good flick to tragedy.

When I started my sabbatical, I felt the temptation to turn on cruise control. The first thing I did when I started my sabbatical was binge-watch *Breaking Bad* all the way through. Yes, that's right. All five seasons and sixty-five episodes. And, yes, it is just as good as everyone says it is.

But after I emerged from the darkness, with dry eyes and crust in the corners of my mouth, I knew I needed to reengage. My routine grew easy, but it wasn't productive.

I couldn't veg out, grow lazy, or forget the set goals—even during my time off. I jumped back into a schedule, read a dozen books, listened more intently in conversations, called wise friends with whom I'd lost touch, and began a more regular exercise regimen.

Every leader must force himself or herself to keep learning regardless of his or her stage of life or career. Change makers lean in, shift their weight forward, and stay hungry even when coasting is infinitely easier. If you're not learning, you're not leading to your full potential. Hall of fame college basketball coach John Wooden said, "A leader who is through learning is through. And so is the team such a leader leads. It's what you learn after you know it all that counts."[1]

If you're not convinced, you could talk to Gerard Seijts, executive director of the Ian O. Ihnatowycz Institute for Leadership. He spent an entire year interviewing thirty-one senior and high-profile leaders. Seijts found that one of the chief characteristics these influencers shared was a commitment to learning.

> 🐦 **IF YOU'RE NOT LEARNING, YOU'RE NOT LEADING TO YOUR FULL POTENTIAL.**

"Good leaders are really the product of a never-ending process of skill and character development," Seijts wrote. "I am now more convinced than ever that good leaders develop through constant learning about their personalities, relationships and careers, not to mention the kind of leader they want to become."[2]

||||||||||||||||||||||||||||||||||||||||||||||||||||||||||||||||||||||||||||||||||||||||||||||||||||||||||||||||||||||||||||||||||||||||||||||||||||||||||||||||||||||

Cultivating a habit of curiosity should be a one-step process: learn. But most of us know this discipline isn't that simple. Deadlines, PTA meetings, church gatherings, neighborhood barbecues, and baseball practices stretch us like a medieval rack. Under the weight of a busy schedule, nurturing curiosity requires creativity and intentionality. Here are some tips for developing this habit in your life.

- **THINK BEFORE YOU ASK**. Ask great questions. As Claude Levi-Strauss commented, "The wise man doesn't give the right answers, he poses the right questions." Questions are critical to curiosity. Asking great questions keeps you informed, in touch, and aware. But how many of us invest time in developing good questions? Most don't, but all should. Set aside ten minutes before your most important meetings to jot down critical questions you would like answered. Make sure they are open ended and seek to uncover new information or explore a new angle. Asking great questions is most often way more strategic than providing great answers.
- **LISTEN MORE THAN YOU TALK**. Move your mouth less, and tune your ears more. Constantly getting better and improving means being quick to hear and slow to speak. Leaders don't learn when they are talking; they learn when listening. The more you listen, the smarter you

become. Get good at creating conversation. Be the person who listens way more than he speaks. Your posture should be that of inquire rather than esquire. Calvin Coolidge had it right, "no man ever listened himself out of a job."

- **SEEK OUT DIFFERENT**. Spending time with people who are unlike you is a learning accelerator. Most leaders, however, huddle with those who are similar to them in pedigree, education, and career field. As Bill Taylor, cofounder of *Fast Company*, wrote, "Ask any educator and they'll agree: We learn the most when we encounter people who are the least like us. Then ask yourself: Don't you spend most of your time with people who are *exactly* like you? Colleagues from the same company, peers from the same industry, friends from the same profession and neighborhood?"[3] Find people who are so different they make you uncomfortable, and then spend more time with them than you'd prefer to.

> 🐦 **LEADERS ARE READERS. IT IS JUST THAT SIMPLE.**

- **SURROUND YOURSELF WITH SMARTS**. Many influencers lead from a place of insecurity. As a result, they often hire people who are less talented or intelligent than they are. If you're the smartest person in the room, after all, you don't have to worry about someone stealing your job or making you look bad. But this creates a staff dynamic where leaders stop learning. Make sure to surround yourself with people who are smarter than you are.

- **LOOK AND LISTEN**. Set aside one audio and one video talk to consume each month. This doesn't require a new slot in your schedule. For example, you can listen on the commute to work or while you're exercising. The only requirement is that the information contained in these talks must be fresh and challenging.

- **READ, ALREADY.** Whenever people tell me, "I don't read," I want to respond with, "Then you can't lead." Leaders are readers. It is just that simple. Set your Internet browser's home page to a content-based site, like TED or CNN. And keep a running list of magazines you are committed to reading regularly. (I like *Inc., Fortune, Wired*, and *Fast Company*.) And read at least one book a month—more if you can. Read liberally—everything you can that is helping you grow and get better.
- **TAKE A LEARNING LUNCH.** Every quarter, schedule a lunch with a leader in another industry whom you admire and can learn from. Commit yourself to listening more than talking. And of course, make sure to come with a list of good questions.
- **ASK THE "CURIOSITY QUESTION"**: At the end of every day, ask yourself, "Have I learned something new today?" If not, do not go to sleep without reading an article, learning a fact, or exploring a topic of interest to you. As time goes on, try to plan the next day's point of growth at the same time.

One of the great memories I have of a Catalyst Conference is a panel discussion with Andy Stanley, John Maxwell, and Erwin McManus during the first ever conference in 2000. Erwin said something profound, and John immediately looked down at Linda, his longtime assistant in the front row, and made a motion as if he was writing, indicating he wanted his Moleskine notebook to capture what Erwin had just said. In front of two thousand young leaders, John demonstrated his desire to learn. Andy Stanley made a great comment later on, and satirically asked John, "Are you going to take notes on my answers as well?" Live as though you'll die tomorrow, and learn as though you'll live forever. Have an insatiable appetite for learning. An urgency that is almost annoying. Seek knowledge as though you thirst for it.

On November 10, 1990, John W. Gardner delivered a speech to McKinsey & Company in Phoenix, Arizona, that would soon become legendary in the history of American business. Gardner was founder of Common Cause and Independent Sector, a Stanford professor, and architect of Lyndon Johnson's Great Society. His talk, titled "Personal Renewal," urged leaders to remain in a constant state of growing, changing, and learning. The enemy of leadership, he said, was boredom.

Gardner said, "You can keep your zest until the day you die. If I may offer you a simple maxim, 'Be interesting.' Everyone wants to be interesting—but the vitalizing thing is to be interested. Keep a sense of curiosity. Discover new things. Care. Risk failure. Reach out."[4]

If you're not growing, you're not going. If you're not learning, you're not leading. And while it is great to be *interesting*, it's more important to be *interested*. Stay curious.

FOUR TIPS ON CURIOSITY FROM BRIAN WURZELL

BRIAN WURZELL IS A WORSHIP LEADER AND PASTOR.

- Ask lots of questions from all kinds of people and then listen! I ask other organizational leaders how they're doing things.
- Pursue generational relationships and let them offer you the gift of experience and wisdom.
- Practice a new spiritual discipline to challenge your life, schedule, and rhythms.
- Find a single leader in the space or place you desire to grow and study them intensely.

MATT CARTER ON CURIOSITY

MATT CARTER IS THE PASTOR OF THE MULTICAMPUS AUSTIN STONE COMMUNITY CHURCH.

I'd recommend several things to leaders who want to develop a habit of curiosity. I'd suggest they find two to three high-quality blogs to follow, to attend one or two of the best conferences in their field, to network with other like-minded innovators, and to read one new book per month.

But all of our best efforts are worthless unless leaders ask God to open them to learning and creating. Innovating requires a teachable spirit and openness to new ideas. God created every human to have some capacity for inventing and creating new things. Even if you don't consider yourself to be creative, there is a part of you that is made to create.

NINE

A HABIT OF PASSION

LOVE WHAT YOU DO

Contrary to the opinions of sports haters out there, it's not all hype. I'm talking about football, and specifically, about Oklahoma Sooners football.

I don't remember much about the first game I attended. I was a youngster, probably around six or seven. The score has escaped my memory, and I can't describe a single play Oklahoma ran. Heck, I don't even know which opponent we played. But I'll still never forget it.

The smell of hot dogs assaulting me like a tractor beam as I walked into Memorial Stadium. The brassy, thumping sound of the band playing "Boomer Sooner" and the way it woke up the crowd. The sea of more than seventy thousand fanatics donning crimson and cream, all sharing an uncommon, almost indescribable bond. Jerseys, painted faces, pom-poms, revelry. If there's anything like Oklahoma football, I've never come across it.

My experience that day planted a seed of passion for Oklahoma football inside of me that has grown over the years. Of course, I went on to attend many more football games at Oklahoma, as a fan, then as a student, and now as a graduate. I sometimes get a chill even now hearing the fight song played through my television speakers. But in recent years, Oklahoma football has become more than a sports obsession for me; it's become a reminder.

It's a reminder that passion for something—sports, faith, a hobby, a relationship—has a way of bonding people and searing memories. That enthusiasm stokes and restokes an internal, unseen fire such that even doing the same thing over and over again never feels old. It's a reminder that passion is critical to sustain long-term interest and zeal in the things we love.

But it's also a reminder that most people aren't passionate about their life's work, and their life's leadership. I rarely feel the same level of energy when I hear people talk about their assignments and careers. Often you'll feel a spark of enthusiasm when someone begins a new venture, but this usually fades over time until the raging bonfire of passion has dwindled to a pile of ashes with a few barely glowing embers. This is an utter shame.

> 🐦 **LEADERS SHOULD BE AS PASSIONATE ABOUT THEIR LIFE'S WORK AS THEY ARE THEIR TOP SPORTS TEAM OR FAVORITE PASTIME.**

Leaders should be as passionate about their life's work as they are their top sports team or favorite pastime. But fervor is not just something that happens; it is also developed. If you do not nurture enthusiasm, it will naturally diminish over time. This is true with friendship and with faith. Most of my married friends tell me this is true of their marriages. And this is certainly true of your assignments, calling, and career.

The need to maintain this passion is even more critical when one considers the contagious nature of passion. When you're excited about the work you're doing, your team is more likely to feed off that emotion. If you love it, your tribe, market, and customers will love it because you love it. Likewise, if you're uninterested or apathetic, your team is less likely to be revved up. Leaders can't inspire others unless and until they are inspired themselves.

We feed off of passionate and contagious leaders. We've all had teachers growing up who were incredibly passionate about their subjects. For me, Mr. Galatian and Mrs. Stephens stand out. Mr. Galatian made me excited about calculus, and Mrs. Stephens fired me up about senior English. They dragged me along kicking and screaming to a level of enthusiasm and excitement about two subjects I really wasn't interested in. Their energy fed my energy, and kept me engaged and excited every day. Your level of passion will pull people along with you. Are you your best customer? Would you be interested in your product, service, or offering if you weren't being paid to sell it?

You have to walk in with a positive attitude and unbridled passion every single day. I learned this a few years ago following a big Catalyst registration deadline day when our team broke a record for the most registrations in one week. In my intensity and ambition, I immediately moved on to the next project while the office buzzed with excitement and energy. Suddenly, I could feel the office's spirit go sour. When I asked my assistant, Michelle, what was going on, she shot straight: "Everyone was hoping you would be excited about the good news and hitting a goal."

Your team feeds off your energy, for better or worse. Your passion gives permission to those around you to express theirs. You may have to push, pull, kick, or gently nudge people, but part of your responsibility as a leader is to show up, every day, with a level of energy, passion, and enthusiasm that elevates your attitude toward constant positivity. You don't have a choice. Leaders are organizational health risks or assets. You've got to love it and live it if you're going to lead it!

When leaders begin to lose their passion, suddenly they question the meaning of their work and whether or not it's time to jump ship. Often they will blame their boss or their coworkers or their organization rather than consider that they haven't been developing a habit of passion. They'll just say things like "I'm bored," "I feel trapped," "I'm not the person I want to be," or "Life's too short."[1]

Want to keep and maintain a high level of passion among your team? Here's how.

- **NAME YOUR WINS.** It's not difficult to think of what went wrong in a day or meeting or project. This comes naturally. But also take time to talk about the victories. "Very often, we let the day to day frustrations cloud the bigger purpose of why we took the job to begin with," says Phil Cooke, a media producer and author of *One Big Thing.* He recommends that you "look at the big picture of what your company's doing and the part you play. Chances are, your position is far more critical than you realize."[2]

- **LEARN TO LOVE.** Every assignment and every season within every assignment is not going to naturally light your fire. Resist the temptation to "just make it through the day" and spend all your free time griping to friends about how terrible your situation is. You don't always get to do what you love; sometimes you have to force yourself to love what you do.[3]

- **MANAGE YOUR EXPECTATIONS.** You must realize that no one else will be as passionate as you are. If you are the founder or executive director or project manager, your job is to pull people up to your level of passion, not let others pull you down. Most won't care as much about what you're working on as you do. Don't expect your team to always match or exceed your passion.

- **TRUST AND RELEASE YOUR EMOTIONS.** Laugh a lot. Cry when the situation warrants it. Don't be afraid to show passion to your team. It's okay to wear your emotions on your sleeve—people like witnessing your humanity.

- **STOP AND RECHARGE**. Sometimes all the ingredients for passion are present, but you're too burnt-out to piece them together. When you've reached the end of your rope, force yourself to stop and take a vacation (or "stay-cation"). You're responsible to reignite the passion light on a regular basis. If you don't recharge, you aren't serving anyone well.

- **GET A COACH**. Even if you're an A+ leader, you can't be an objective observer of yourself. Find someone with experience leading leaders, and invite him or her into the process. Often a good leadership coach can help pry you from your slump. Find a mentor or leaders inside and outside your industry to connect with. Visit other organizations. They may confirm that it isn't you and it's time to look for a new assignment.

When I think of passion, I envision the "blue shirters" who work at the Apple store. Every time I walk into one of these retail locations, there's an energy. It's almost buzzing, and it's not just the sound of the computers running. People are genuinely excited to be there. I imagine none of them are becoming millionaires helping customers, and yet they have found a way to love what they do. Most of them aren't just there because they need a job. They are passionate about their work, and they are heroes to me. In fact, many times I'll make a purchase or decide to jump in on a new Apple product just because of the energy and passion of the blue shirters. Their passion

> 🐦 **YOU DON'T ALWAYS GET TO DO WHAT YOU LOVE; SOMETIMES YOU HAVE TO FORCE YOURSELF TO LOVE WHAT YOU DO.**

for the product they are selling creates passion in me for the product they are selling.

Whether you are wearing crimson in Memorial Stadium or blue in an Apple store or just putting on a charcoal blazer for an 8 a.m. presentation, passion is critical to doing your best work and enjoying it along the way. Your life's work is too important not to love what you do.

MARK BATTERSON ON PASSION

MARK BATTERSON IS PASTOR OF NATIONAL COMMUNITY CHURCH AND BESTSELLING AUTHOR OF *THE CIRCLE MAKER*.

A professor in seminary asked me, "What makes you cry or pound your fist on the table?" In other words, he wanted me to identify what made me sad or mad. He knew that would reveal what is probably a God-ordained passion that I needed to tap into.

One of my core convictions is: there are ways of doing church that no one has thought of yet. That idea gets me up early and keeps me up late. So one way I stay passionate is keeping my head, heart, and hands in new endeavors—whether that's writing a book or launching our next campus. Passion feeds off our natural inclinations. Once you know what you're passionate about, you need to feed it.

FOUR TIPS ON PASSION FROM SAMUEL RODRIGUEZ

SAMUEL RODRIGUEZ IS PRESIDENT OF THE NATIONAL HISPANIC CHRISTIAN LEADERSHIP CONFERENCE.

Passion does not stem from our cognitive domain; passion emerges out of our spirit. When God's presence saturates our daily lives, *then* passion arises. In order to facilitate passion, I engage in the following daily activities:

- **PASSIONATE PRAYER**: By praying passionately for righteousness, God's will to be done, and the needs of those who suffer, I become a more passionate person.
- **PASSIONATE WORSHIP**: By understanding that there is no such thing as comfortable Christianity and that Jesus seeks those who worship him in spirit and truth, I daily commit to worshipping the Lamb with passion and purpose.

- **PASSIONATE PROCLAMATION**: Daily, I proclaim the truth of Christ with love to those around me and to those God places before me. I ask God to order my steps so that all my actions, words, and thoughts proclaim the good news.
- **PASSIONATE ACTIVISM**: I seek to quench the thirst, feed the hunger, and welcome "the stranger" in Jesus' name.

THOUGHTS ON PASSION FROM AMENA BROWN OWEN

AMENA BROWN OWEN IS A SPOKEN WORD ARTIST, CREATIVE, AND AUTHOR OF *BREAKING OLD RHYTHMS*.

I pay attention to what I'm passionate about and make sure I'm doing that several times a week. For me, that's creativity, music, art, writing, and [the] spoken word. I also listen to music that motivates and inspires me. I make playlists for waking up, working out, and writing that make me dance, think, and want to create.

Take time off. When I'm tired and burnt out it's hard to lead with passion, so I have to make sure I unplug and rest. I also fuel my passion by connecting with others living out theirs. Once a week I schedule a coffee with a friend, writer, artist, or colleague to hear their stories and be inspired to live out mine.

Find a way to do more of the things that make you want to stay up late and get up early to work on. Take classes or workshops that awaken your creativity. Create a list of your childhood passions. Childhood passions many times connect to adult habits.

A HABIT OF INNOVATION

STAY CURRENT, CREATIVE, AND ENGAGED

If you played a word association game with *Catalyst*, many people in our community would say "creative." The organization has always been considered innovative. It never settles for average, and is always trying to outdo itself. To forge new paths, to utilize new technology, and to stay fresh.

Many leaders today assume that creativity is an inborn quality. When I consult with leaders about innovation, they will often interrupt me: "Oh, I'm not a creative." It is one of those characteristics that some people suppose is woven into your DNA or is totally missing from your makeup.

There's about half a teaspoon of truth in this. Some people *are* naturally creative. Andy Warhol didn't make a conscious decision to learn how to create groundbreaking pop art while he was punching a calculator in an accounting firm cubicle. Jonathan Ive naturally had a creative eye for designing some of the most creative products ever at Apple. Many people—musicians and novelists, painters and poets, designers and graphic artists—ended up with an extra helping of creativity at birth. But the rest of us aren't just out of luck. We can nurture a spirit of innovation in ourselves and our organizations.

I say "us" because I'm not naturally creative. People are often surprised when I tell them this, since I led such an innovative organization. I don't draw out my thoughts in abstract art with colored pencils. You won't catch me lying in a poppy field, writing poetry. I'm naturally logical. I think in systems. I have an almost unhealthy love for creating lists.

But as I learned while working at Catalyst, creativity is not completely inborn. It's not just the musician sitting on the rooftop, dreaming up new lyrics about the color of the sky at noontime. It is the man in the third third of his life, taking a college course to learn more about his field. It is the CEO who schedules a lunch with a local graphic designer to talk about trends in logo design. It is the team of accountants who train themselves to use a revolutionary computer program before anyone else in their market does. The key to innovation is intentionality.

> **THE KEY TO INNOVATION IS INTENTIONALITY.**

Innovation takes work. Lots of work. *Hard* work. Energy and preparation are critical. Bestselling author and Barna Group president David Kinnaman says, "True creativity comes from disciplined habits." Even the most creative leaders don't just show up and flip the innovation switch on and start pumping out paradigm-shifting, world-changing ideas. The reason certain groups and organizations are ultimately more creative than others is that their leaders are *intentional* when it comes to creating environments where creativity can flourish. It is not because their CEO or department heads were born creative. Innovation is up to you.

Innovation matters, and true leadership requires innovation. Leadership is not management. Managing is creating expected results with constraints. Managers can be leaders, and leaders can be managers.

A leader is a change agent. He or she changes the order of things and pushes for change. Leadership is not about title or position or a corner office or a big budget. Or power. Leaders imagine a different future and change the order of things, regardless of title or position. I realized this a few years ago when I began (predictably) making a list of all the basic components that comprise innovation. As I broke down this characteristic, I realized intentionality is made up of at least four elements:

Courage: Innovation requires a willingness to accept risk and step out into uncertainty.

Failure: Innovation almost never happens on the first try. It requires at least one—and usually multiple—disappointments.

Stamina: Innovation occurs at the end of the process, not the beginning. The most creative idea is almost never the first suggested. Innovative leaders learn to push through their quitting points. Often, we abandon a process right before a breakthrough would have occurred.

Spark: Innovation happens when we create moments and space conducive to birthing new ideas. You may not be naturally creative, but if you're willing to get the right people in the right room at the right time, ignition can occur.

Most leaders I meet who claim to be devoid of creativity are shocked when I break down innovation into its base elements. As it turns out, even leaders who aren't naturally creative can be, with a little work. Opportunities for innovation are all around us. There are always new and better ways to do what one is currently doing. But you have to be willing to do the work necessary to discover it. "You will never stumble upon the unexpected if you stick only to the familiar," wrote Ed Catmull, the cofounder of Pixar, constantly ranked as one of the most innovative companies in the world.

Innovation is the opposite of average. It is refusing to coast, rejecting the status quo, and having the courage to shake up the meaningless routines that lead to laziness. Innovation is the act of exploring new ideas, and every leader must develop this habit in his own life if he wants to become a change maker. Innovators are authentic voices, not just echo chambers. Too many organizations, conferences, leaders, and communities are just copycats of someone else. Be unique and stand out. To improve is to change; to be perfect is to change often, said Winston Churchill.

The first step to developing this habit is realizing that innovation in part has nothing to do with you; rather, it is determined by those you have around you. One of the secrets to making Catalyst an industry leader in creativity was our willingness to recruit innovative leaders. Every time I searched for a new employee, I sought a person who was naturally innovative. This made a difference on several occasions, in ways both large and small.

A few years ago, one of my team members came to me with a fresh idea. He wanted to nix the Excel spreadsheets we were using to organize our event schedules, programming, and production. He had an intuition that there was a more innovative way to organize this, and by doing a little research, discovered a software program that connected everyone to the same system. Multiple people could be working on the same program sheet at the same time. Everyone was updated in real time. The program even had templates that were customizable to our needs as event producers.

I'm sorry to say that I dismissed him. Not wanting to change, I resisted the thought of embracing a new system. For months he continued to urge me, but I tumbled deeper into the "if it ain't broke, don't fix it" trap. He was being innovative, and I wasn't.

I resisted it because I didn't want to change. I should have realized that even if something "ain't broke," it can still be improved. We found something that worked; why should we change? Finally, I agreed to use the software, and it made everyone's job faster, more efficient, and just downright better. It actually created margin for us to brainstorm new ideas and plan moments of surprise for which we otherwise wouldn't have had time. Looking back, I wish I had been more open at the beginning. Thankfully, I had an innovator on my team who was willing to keep pushing.

Catalyst also included innovative outsiders and consultants in our creative process. We brought in people like Jeff Shinabarger and Carlos Whittaker, Lanny Donoho, Reggie Joiner, Ryan Shove, Amena Brown Owen, Tripp Crosby, and Tyler Stanton, whose hands shaped our organization significantly over the years. They joined and often led brainstorming sessions where there were no restrictions and where failure was encouraged. I can't even begin to quantify the difference this made.

> 🐦 **INNOVATION IN PART HAS NOTHING TO DO WITH YOU; RATHER, IT IS DETERMINED BY THOSE YOU HAVE AROUND YOU.**

Who are the innovators on your team? Have you been intentional to scatter naturally creative people throughout your ranks? If not, can you commit to that in the future? And can you start now looking for innovative outsiders to include in your creative processes?

Answering questions like these will determine whether you will become an innovative influencer or mundane manager. Innovation is failing over and over until it works. The guy who invented the ship also invented the shipwreck, says Seth Godin.

Creativity can be exhausting because it is a process, not an act. Today's cutting-edge products, systems, software, and technologies will be passé tomorrow. When you innovate, don't idolize or your most imaginative ventures will cannibalize your creativity.

Many years ago, our team dreamed up the "Catalyst Filter." This subscription-based product was a box that arrived in the mail on a regular basis. Inside, customers would find a selection of items intended to challenge, encourage, and equip our network of influencers. Our team had a blast curating a selection of invitations to members-only events, advance copies of books, exclusive articles, and sometimes even a whimsical toy just for fun. It was also a way to deliver the Catalyst experience to them between events. It was well designed with high-quality materials and created a "surprise and delight" moment for the recipient. Think Birchbox for Christian leaders.

> **WHEN YOU INNOVATE, DON'T IDOLIZE OR YOUR MOST IMAGINATIVE VENTURES WILL CANNIBALIZE YOUR CREATIVITY.**

The product was immediately popular as people recognized the freshness of our idea. But over time, one of our most-innovative ideas ran the risk of becoming stale and commonplace. We found ourselves less interested in the Catalyst Filter and tempted to just fill each box with the same type of goods. Anyone who suggested revamping it was met with resistance. Our most imaginative venture threatened to make us *less* creative as it became a routine. The thing that once spurred innovation ran the risk of becoming a swamp we'd get stuck in.

Luckily, our team recognized this early on. We knew that our people expected a better experience each time they received a new box in the mail (warning: once you start innovating, you are on the hook). Continuing to produce the Filter as it had been was not an option. And we began working to revamp the product regularly, challenging ourselves to take it in new directions, and soliciting outside advice from inventive thinkers.

Ever heard of Dick Fosbury? He changed the trajectory of an entire sport with his new and creative way to high-jump, appropriately titled the "Fosbury Flop," still in vogue today. Innovation has changed the music industry, moving from records to cassettes to CDs and now digital downloads. The iPhone and iPad changed technology. Creativity and innovation positively move the ball down the field, and require leaders willing to change, because leaders change things.

> 🐦 **CREATIVITY CAN BE EXHAUSTING BECAUSE IT IS NOT AN ACT, BUT A PROCESS.**

The moral of this story is that developing a habit of innovation requires intentional, systemic processes and attention to the rhythms of your life and workdays. Following are some practices that have worked well for the teams I've led:

1. **PUT YOUR MONEY WHERE YOUR INNOVATIVE MOUTH IS.** I can usually tell a lot about an individual's or an organization's true commitment to creativity just by reviewing their finances. Simply put: if you're not investing in innovation, then it is not a priority. You should set aside funds for you and your team to take like-minded innovators out to lunch on occasion, and encourage every team member to attend at least one professional development conference per year. And these are only for starters. As time goes on, you should invest an increasing amount of money in creative ventures. These will pay dividends in employee satisfaction and product enhancements.

2. **SHAKE THINGS UP.** Make changes often to avoid staleness in any way. Move around where people sit in the office, change the times when meetings are "usually" held, or alter the dress code. On the last one, I don't mean make

people wear ties for no reason. Rather, implement fun and unique suggestions. Perhaps one week you might ask everyone to wear at least one polka-dotted item. Changing perspective can shift trajectory. Football teams can change the direction of an entire game just by bringing in the backup quarterback. It's amazing how small shifts can cultivate a culture where change is embraced. Change is our friend, because change reflects growth and creates healthy tension, and out of healthy tension true clarity tends to emerge.

3. **KEEP THE FUN FACTOR HIGH.** Business that's all business isn't the best business. Provide your team with "innovation enhancers," such as toys, balls, candy, and even noisemakers from time to time. Also, remember that a meeting's vibe is crucial. Music and atmosphere are critical to creativity. There should always be energetic lighting, piles of snacks, and endless coffee and caffeinated drinks (no one brainstorms well while sleeping).

4. **MOVE.** Physical motion is a creativity accelerator. Every sixty minutes of meeting time needs at least ten minutes of motion. Encourage people to stand up, walk around, or even have a micro dance party! Also, urge people to move throughout the day. (Walking or running meetings are an acquired taste, but quite beneficial to some.) And this should also be a part of your personal routine. If you aren't exercising, then start. Run, swim, bike, join a baseball league, or climb a mountain. Do something to keep moving and get your creative juices flowing.

5. **FIND REASONS TO SAY YES.** Many high-level leaders are the masters of "no." But the *best* ones are architects of "yes." You should find ways to give people the green light

as much as possible. An employee wants to take a day to work from a mountaintop? "Yes." Someone suggests Skyping in an innovator from Hong Kong to a meeting? "Yes." Team members request having chocolate cheese-cake at the next product development meeting? "Yes." You get the point. Open as many doors as possible, and see if innovation doesn't walk through a few of them.

6. **CREATE BOUNDARIES.** Most leaders think they must give the creatives on their team lots and lots of room to be creative. But this is not true. Borders and boundaries are good for creatives. After all, pictures have frames. So let your creatives paint with broad perspective, but in focused areas. Build riverbanks in which the creative water can run. Hillsong executive pastor Joel A'Bell says, "Life without boundaries is a life without freedom."

7. **KEEP GOING.** Most teams give up too quickly on ideas because they feel "stuck." But being stuck is usually a mile marker on the way to greatness. Most new ideas and innovations don't work out the way you hoped. But with persistence and continual improvement, great ideas can be born. YouVersion is a great example of this. Originally meant as a website, the idea was almost scrapped, but Bobby Gruenewald decided to try it out as an app before scrapping the project. Now, more than 150 million people around the world use YouVersion as their go-to Bible app on their phones and tablets.

8. **MAKE MEETINGS CREATIVE.** Meetings are (sadly) where most business happens. So they need to be innovation fac-tories. Here are four rules for crafting creative meetings:

   a. *Include outsiders*: Invite like-minded innovators from outside your team to join you on occasion. Some in-fluencers avoid this practice because they don't want to inconvenience others, but in my experience, most creative people like attending brainstorming meetings because they know it will invigorate them.

b. *Exclude (some) insiders*: Not everyone should be invited to brainstorming meetings or asked to participate in the creative process. Be wary of including people who work in finance, for example, who always raise the objection that "we can't afford this" before the idea is even fleshed out. Unless they can think outside the box, keep the bean counters away. And if someone says, "But that's not the way we've always done it," they are immediately banned from the next meeting. Debbie Downer and Mr. "No" aren't invited. And don't feel bad when they get mad.

c. *Allow for rabbit trails*: Though your team must always move projects in a certain direction, make time to explore unrelated ideas. Additionally, tease out the seemingly mediocre ideas when brainstorming. Often, the best idea was an "average" idea that was given time to marinate.

d. *Take very detailed notes*: Find the least creative person in the office who wants to be involved and make him or her the note taker. This role is crucial. Make sure your note taker captures everything that is said and created. Capturing ideas and then being able to retrieve them later is crucial. Everyone thinks they can remember the best ideas, but they'll be forgotten within hours if not minutes. Notes help you implement innovation.

Implementing these practices will help you develop a habit of innovation. And don't worry about overdoing it and somehow making your team *too* creative. It is much easier to slow down a racehorse by pulling back on the reins than motivating a field horse by spurring and kicking and pleading. So giddyup and get started. Or, as President Jimmy Carter once said, "Go out on a limb. That's where the fruit is."

🐦 **IF YOU'RE NOT INVESTING IN INNOVATION, THEN IT IS NOT A PRIORITY.**

No one likes to fail. No one. But as leaders developing a habit of innovation, we must allow for it. In fact, we must embrace it. Failure is crucial for innovation to actually become second nature for a team. If you're not failing, you're not risking enough. Give yourself and those around you permission to make mistakes. Embrace failure as a step forward process. Reality is, all of your ideas are not great. In fact, 90 percent are probably bad and doomed to fail. Five percent are decent. And maybe 5 percent are great. To get to the one in twenty that are great, you have to have another nineteen that fail. *One* in twenty. Failures are scars on the way to ultimate success. Your failure scars reveal your success identity.

In fact, you should create an environment that rewards forward-leaning innovation and failure. Don't just reward failure for failure's sake. That will frustrate your high achievers. But forward leaning means you are doing everything you can to deliver a home run. Innovation is best achieved by fearless organizations. You reward what matters most. And reward leads to repetition. What is rewarded gets repeated.

For a good example of innovation, head a little more than an hour east of my home to Athens, Georgia. There you'll find a bustling college town that the Red Dress Boutique calls home. This venture was founded by Diana Harbour in 2005 as a traditional brick-and-mortar clothing store for women. Before opening Red Dress, Harbour had been churning out brochure copy for a financial services firm while she daydreamed of a more creative venture.

When Red Dress opened, sales were slow. So Harbour began imagining new ways to generate revenue. She started with Facebook, which was in its early days, using her husband's college e-mail address to gain access. But the Red Dress page was shut down three times because the site didn't have company pages at the time. In 2007, the ban lifted and Harbour leaned into social media completely.

She set up Twitter and Instagram profiles, established Facebook and Pinterest pages, and even jumped on Wanelo. She began sharing images of her at market and let customers peek into the life of a boutique owner, and even set up a VIP page where the most loyal shoppers can talk directly to her when she is on a buying trip.

Harbour even dabbled in custom photography to make her social media pages as fresh as her boutique's website. She recruited student models and shot them outdoors on the streets of Athens to give customers a sense of how the garments can be worn in everyday life. Oh, and when the garment arrives, it is accompanied by a handwritten thank-you note and surprise free merchandise.

Harbour's willingness to get online and get social early on in addition to her ability to test new and better strategies have catapulted her venture to success. Red Dress has grown their sales from $63,000 in 2010 to more than $7 million. Online sales comprise 93 percent of this revenue. Their warehouse space has expanded from thirty-five hundred square feet to forty-five thousand.[1]

Today, she is still dreaming. She solicits advice from models on how to take better photographs. She is working with designers to create a better website and mainframe. And she's even developing a private-label clothing line. Innovators, like e-commerce, never stop.

And if you want to develop this habit, you shouldn't either. Be willing to try new things, to press into the unknown. Stay up on the latest trends in your field, and be in constant conversation with others who are succeeding. Embrace risk; embrace change; embrace failure; and most of all, have fun.

SIX TIPS ON INNOVATION FROM CHARLES LEE

CHARLES LEE IS CEO OF IDEATION AND AUTHOR OF *GOOD IDEA. NOW WHAT?*

If someone wanted to be more innovative in their life, I would encourage them to . . .

- View innovation as an act of problem-solving.
- Nurture their skills in identifying core issues around problems.
- Think in terms of tangible pathways for designing potential solutions to solve these problems.
- Document progress on innovation and determine criteria for success in this area.
- Hire smart, passionate, curious, talented creatives.
- Don't wait on things to happen; make things happen.

SIX TIPS ON INNOVATION FROM CASS LANGTON

CASS LANGTON IS THE GLOBAL CREATIVE PASTOR OF HILLSONG CHURCH.

To be more innovative, I suggest leaders spend an hour a week on these types of behaviors:

- **THE "THREE DIFFERENT WAYS" EXERCISE:** When you're faced with a problem, try solving it three different ways.
- **READ WIDER:** Encounter different genres than you would usually be drawn to online and in print.
- **LISTEN WIDER:** This includes different genres of music, podcasts, and audio books.

- **CHANGE UP WHAT YOU DO AND WHERE YOU GO:** Walk different routes, go to galleries, shows, movies, or even just drink coffee in different places.
- **KEEP A FOLIO OF IDEAS:** Sleep with a notebook by your bed for your late-night inspiration.
- **GUARD YOUR HEART.** Grow your capacity. Be generous with your praise. Work hard.

ELEVEN

A HABIT OF INSPIRATION

NURTURE A VISION FOR A BETTER TOMORROW

The world was watching in anticipation as Barack Obama delivered his 2008 acceptance speech in Chicago. Those who campaigned for him, who voted for him, choked back tears or let them stream down their cheeks. Even many who did not vote for him, who opposed his vision for governing America, recount that they felt a certain sense of pride that their country had elected an African American to the highest office in the land.

Some would say that the lifeblood of Barack Obama's campaign was not the candidate's limited record or even his policy proposals for how to reform our government. It was the promise of "hope" and "change," a vision that resonated with millions and led to a landslide victory.

Whether Barack Obama delivered on his promises is a matter of debate, but the election of the forty-fourth president teaches us an important lesson: people long to be a part of something bigger than themselves. We want to alter the future, to set our gaze on tomorrow, to believe that life can be better than it is today, to hope. This is part of what it means to be human.

Recognizing this core part of the human spirit can help struggling leaders soar to new heights. A vision for the future makes work meaningful. It makes work enjoyable. It makes getting out of bed at 6 a.m. and arriving home after dinner "worth it." People need to be motivated, and casting a vision that propels them forward is one of the first and central tasks of a leader today. Hope is true currency for this generation.

> 🐦 **PEOPLE NEED TO BE MOTIVATED, AND CASTING A VISION THAT PROPELS THEM FORWARD IS ONE OF THE FIRST AND CENTRAL TASKS OF A LEADER.**

Of course, you can't inspire people to a vision if you don't have one. The statement is almost too simple to say, but it's true. Many leaders don't inspire their people because they don't have anything inspirational to say. Influencers who want to develop a habit of inspiration must craft a captivating vision for the future and a persuasive plan for how to get there. People won't willingly follow until they can see how they share in the future you envision.

According to leadership research conducted by authors Jim Kouzes and Barry Posner, "Being forward-looking is the quality that most separates leaders from individual contributors . . . [But] it's something that too few fully appreciate, and too many devote almost no time to developing."[1]

I remember my first time driving a car, which was a dusty, rusty feed truck in rural Oklahoma. Sitting on a Tulsa phone book so I could see over the dash and also reach the gas pedal, I learned that reaching the destination meant looking ahead through the windshield, not looking through the rearview mirror. It's hard to move forward by looking at where you've been. You have to focus on what's in front of you. Race car drivers know this—if they look at the wall, they will hit the wall. They must focus on the track in front of them.

So let's begin at the beginning. If you haven't developed a vision statement for both you and your organization . . . what are you waiting on? Seriously. Put this book down and work on that. It's more important. If you have a vision statement, make sure it is an effective one. It needs to focus the energy of your work, hone in on what you're about, prioritize your passions, and create energy among those it intends to motivate. The best vision statements have the following qualities:

- **THEY ARE *OPTIMISTIC*:** One of the chief functions of a vision statement is to motivate. When you draft yours, step back and ask, "Does this paint a picture of tomorrow that fills me with hope?" The answer must be yes. If your organization exists to combat a global injustice or to improve a serious marketplace flaw, make sure it devotes more words to the solution than to the problem.

  Great leaders have double vision. It is focused like a microscope, but is far-reaching like a telescope. You must have both. Make sure your vision statement focuses on the now but yearns for what is next and possible. As former secretary of state Colin Powell once said, "optimism is a force multiplier."

- **THEY ARE *SIMPLE*:** If your vision statement takes more than five minutes to memorize, it's too complicated. If it has bullet points, it needs refinement. If it contains words that require the hearer to reference a dictionary, grab a thesaurus and find some synonyms that simplify. The simpler a vision statement is, the more profound, powerful, and potent it can be.

- **THEY ARE *PERSONAL*:** People will work for other people in a way they will not work for anything else. As leadership guru Dan Rockwell wrote, "Vision always centers on people, never projects, programs, properties, or profits."[2] Make sure your statement isn't loaded down in industry jargon or focused on technical elements of business.

- **THEY ARE *FLEXIBLE*:** Though a vision statement can benefit from a level of specificity, it should be flexible enough to allow for the changes that will inevitably come with time. As new technologies arise, marketplace trends emerge, or your business model adjusts, this statement should still work. When a vision statement is flexible, it will be liberating instead of limiting.

If you want a good example of a compelling vision statement, survey the nonprofit world. This sector tends to be naturally optimistic and visionary. Make-A-Wish's website says, "Our vision is that people everywhere will share the power of a wish." World Wildlife Federation's statement is, "We seek to save a planet, a world of life. Reconciling the needs of human beings and the needs of others that share the Earth." Kiva's says, "We envision a world where all people—even in the most remote areas of the globe— hold the power to create opportunity for themselves and others."

If you want a strong example from the business world, look no further than Amazon's mission statement: "Our vision is to be earth's most customer centric company; to build a place where people can come to find and discover anything they might want to buy online."

> 🐦 **WHEN A VISION STATEMENT IS FLEXIBLE, IT WILL BE LIBERATING INSTEAD OF LIMITING.**

Once a leader gets a few wins under his belt, he faces the temptation to grow complacent. Resist this at all costs. It will breed dissatisfaction with your life and work. Instead, craft a vision that excites you and your team and then work hard to make it reality. When you are tempted to settle for whatever life has handed you, develop a vision for creating a better tomorrow.

A habit of inspiration is nurtured in the casting, not just the crafting of vision. Once leaders discover and develop their vision, they learn to communicate it regularly and clearly. Leaders who don't communicate their vision are no better off than leaders who have no vision to communicate.

No one wakes up wanting to be managed. We wake up wanting to be led. We walk into an office or are part of a team ultimately because we hope and want to believe that we are making a difference. "If you hire people just because they can do a job, they'll work for your money. But if you hire people who believe what you believe, they'll work for you with blood and sweat and tears," tweeted author and motivational speaker Simon Sinek. We want to be part of an adventure, we desire to make a mark, and we long to be part of something significant that stretches and astonishes us. Inspiring leaders create a vision, mission, and cause way bigger than themselves that others can own, follow, be inspired by, and be a part of. Pastor Louie Giglio, of Passion City Church, says, "The stakes are too high for us to die with a small vision."

> 🐦 **LEADERS WHO DON'T COMMUNICATE THEIR VISION ARE NO BETTER OFF THAN LEADERS WHO HAVE NO VISION TO COMMUNICATE.**

Ritz Carlton employees know the power of a powerful vision. The high-end hotel chain provides a powerful and inspiring picture of what they expect from their employees: they are "ladies and gentlemen serving ladies and gentlemen." For their frontline staff, such as housekeeping, maintenance, and front desk employees, this is a life-giving vision for how they conduct them-selves. They are empowered to make a difference in the lives of hotel guests, providing dignity, purpose and relevancy—giving evidence of the notion that when a vision is strong enough, it's not that you have a vision; it's that the vision has you.[3]

Inspiration can even capture an entire city. Oklahoma City recently lost one million pounds. That's right, forty-seven thou-sand local residents participated in a citywide campaign to get fit. A vision that tomorrow will be better than today, and even something so personal as losing weight, can be a citywide initiative. This was a level of inspiration that not only built new lifestyle habits, but also reduced waistlines.[4]

Here are ways to develop a habit and create a culture of inspiration:

- **INVITE PARTICIPATION.** Vision should never be forced upon, shackled to, or mandated to people. You and your people must buy into it. Look for opportunities to invite a wide swath of people into the vision-crafting and vision-casting processes. If you're developing or refining your vision statement, ask for input across your entire team. If you're brainstorming ways to better disseminate it, seek the help of the most competent communicators around you. The more people speak into the process, the more people will respect the product. Ask yourself—are you creating an environment and culture where people on your team can be big? Or are you holding them back and forcing them to be small?
- **TELL STORIES.** Stories move people and parable is para-mount. Humans connect with stories in ways we don't connect with stats, slogans, or statements. So inspira-tional leaders must also be good storytellers. Paint a

picture of a world in which the vision has been realized. And tell stories of those who've helped move the organization and its stakeholders a step closer to that reality. Before long, you'll notice your team will start retelling these tales among themselves. And a few will become legends. Storytelling is authoritative and powerful today. You must inspire as well as inform.

- **STRETCH THE LIMITS.** The vision should compel you to greatness, rather than your greatness compelling the vision. Dream big. Have such a powerful and inspiring vision that it is just short of annoying to those around you, and just short of scary to you and your team. I love how Brad Cooper, student pastor at NewSpring Church, has built one of the largest and most impactful student ministries in the United States. This past summer they took over six thousand students to their own summer camp, which most never thought possible from a rural church in Anderson, South Carolina. And Brad would say they are just getting started.
- **INCENTIVIZE PROGRESS.** People don't achieve goals just because it makes them feel good. They also need a pay-off. What types of incentives are you offering to those who are helping promote your organization's vision? Free tickets, event registrations, books, resources credits, gifts, days off, or even trips are good examples.
- **ENCOURAGE IMPROVEMENT.** Your employees aren't cogs in a corporate wheel. When people propel or exhibit the vision, give them credit. Thank them. Honor them. Encourage them. When people know that you care about them—even more than profits—and appreciate their contributions, they'll lean into the vision. Always be on the lookout for people who are doing things right, and recognize it.

- **HIRE DREAMERS.** You are the chief, but not the only, vision caster. When you hire new team members, don't only staff executers. Stack your roster with some dreamers too. They'll take the vision you're placing in front of them and will run with it. Make sure to ask questions designed to reveal how much time they spend dreaming each day.

- **EXECUTE ANYWAY.** Even as you're nurturing and disseminating your vision, you need to keep forging ahead. I often encourage people to take a "big vision, small aim" approach. Paint pictures, tell stories, draft statements, and motivate your people constantly. But while you wait for people to latch onto these sweeping ideals, stay focused on your customers, team, and targets. Be a big dreamer but someone who can still execute in small ways to move your team forward.

- **EVALUATE REGULARLY.** While many leaders scrutinize the organization's vision itself, few regularly evaluate how well it is being communicated. Conduct an annual review of your team. Ask them to describe the vision that has been set for your organization, department, and subgroups. Evaluate the parity between their answers. This will tell you if you have defined and communicated your vision to them.

I am a type A, "get it done" kind of person. I'm more executer than dreamer. While the skills I naturally possess are critical, most people would rather work for a visionary—someone who can inspire and challenge and confront and compel.

Make sure you're a vision caster and vision catcher, and not a vision snatcher. Cast and catch. Don't snatch. Creating, casting, and carrying the vision is everyone's responsibility, but vision snatchers will kill progress and diffuse momentum.

If I owned a time machine, I'd go back and develop a compelling vision early in each assignment. Then I would find creative ways to reinforce it in the minds of my teams. My tendency is to focus on execution, and let intensity dominate and permeate the culture instead of inspiration. But leaders must be positive, upbeat, and optimistic. Your energy and enthusiasm set the tone. Had I done this, I believe I would have been much more successful as a leader.

Someone who did this right was Wendy Kopp, who founded Teach For America in 1989. She birthed the idea as a cash-strapped college student with nothing more than a vision to "eliminate educational inequities." As part of her senior project, Kopp dreamed about engaging her generation involved with poverty and education by creating a national teaching corps. Many people thought she was crazy—even one of Kopp's academic advisors called it "quite evidently deranged." Why would graduates of America's top schools give up years of their lives to work in the country's highest-need schools for little pay?

Kopp clung to her vision despite the discouragement of her peers and colleagues. She raised more than $2.5 million in seed investments and began recruiting teachers. Today, eleven thousand Teach For America corp members are engaged in the program, working to improve our nation's worst schools. And Kopp now leads Teach For All, an organization working to apply the same vision on a global scale.

The story of Teach For America's birth is a case study in the power of a vision to inspire hope in others and drive an idea forward into reality. You must help your people see beyond what is in front of them. Help them stand on their tiptoes and gaze over the next hill. Motivate them to dream of ways their work can create a better tomorrow. Soon you'll find you aren't just inspiring an employee; you're also inventing a future.

SERGIO DE LA MORA ON INSPIRATION

SERGIO DE LA MORA IS THE FOUNDER AND PASTOR OF
CORNERSTONE CHURCH IN SAN DIEGO.

Casting vision means giving people hope of a preferred future. Of course, vision is more than hope. Hope is the suggestion of something, but vision is the declaration of something. Hope is the suggestion of something that could be, but vision is saying, "this is what is going to be."

Hope is a suggestion, but vision is a declaration of a preferred future.

Because it is so active, vision casting can be exhausting. It has to be cast constantly, but the frequency depends on which season you're in. In a transition season, you have to cast vision more often. When your organization lacks clarity, you have to cast it more often. In crisis and chaos and change and growth, you have to constantly cast vision. A visionary leader has to know when to cast vision.

THREE TIPS ON INSPIRATION FROM CHAD VEACH

CHAD VEACH IS THE PASTOR OF ZOE CHURCH IN LOS ANGELES.

There are multiple ways to become a visionary, but here are a few important ones . . .

- **GO TO THE VISION GIVER:** Vision comes from God; go to Him.
- **EXPOSE YOURSELF TO VISION:** One of the things that helps me catch a vision is being around people of great vision.
- **TAKE "THINKING TIME":** God told Habakkuk to "write down the vision." [See Habakkuk 2:2 KJV.] You should regularly set aside time to sit down with pen and paper to process what's in your heart. Dreaming about what God has already given me always helps me become a greater visionary.

JON GORDON ON INSPIRATION

JON GORDON IS A BESTSELLING AUTHOR AND LEADERSHIP CONSULTANT.

If someone wants to be more inspirational as a leader, they must first set an example of what inspiration looks like. By living it out, they will inspire those around them. They should lead with optimism, belief, and faith. Inspirational people encourage, coach, mentor, and believe in others more than they believe in themselves. They paint a positive vision for the future and rally and encourage people toward it. They also serve and sacrifice. So I encourage leaders to model inspiration and join [their] team in the trenches and find ways to serve and help them do their best work.

TWELVE

A HABIT OF BRAVERY

TAKE CALCULATED RISKS

When I arrived at the end of my sabbatical, I made the unnerving decision to not return to my previous role of leading Catalyst. I knew a new day was dawning in my life, but I lacked clarity on my next assignment. What would I do next? Where would I go?

During a road trip to Nashville, I called a friend and expressed my unease.

"Why don't you just do your own thing for a while?" he asked. "You could consult with multiple clients and share what you've learned about organizational leadership."

I dismissed the suggestion.

The "consultant lifestyle" had never appealed to me. I'm not a lone-ranger kind of leader. Working with a team invigorates me. Having others around me comforts and challenges me. I'm more intrapreneur than entrepreneur; I enjoy being a rebel from within an organization rather than launching out on my own.

The next week another friend made a similar suggestion. The next week two more joined the chorus. Suddenly, people I respected and who knew me were all offering the same advice independent of each other. I decided to give it serious consideration.

On the one hand, his advice made sense. I had two decades of experience in marketing, branding, strategy, management, and event production. I had amassed a coveted collection of contacts, enjoy traveling, and knew of many who could benefit from leadership coaching and consulting. Why not share my knowledge and philosophy with others?

And yet, starting my own venture was quite the gamble. Having just left an organization in its prime, I was currently a commodity. But if I launched my own endeavor and it flopped, I might not recover. This could ruin me.

I'm a big believer in taking risks, but it was difficult to take my own medicine with so much on the line. It wasn't swimming with great whites, but it did require embracing the unknown. And no one likes to do that. Anxiety swirled. Prayers rolled. Time ticked. Everyday bravery wavered.

Finally, I jumped. I called my accountant and set up an official LLC. A month later, I received a large envelope with paperwork notifying me that "BLINC Consulting" was a real business. Holding the notice in my hand, I thought to myself, *I'm always telling others to live courageously. I guess this is what it feels like.*

Today, I have a steady stream of clients I work with. I'm still more comfortable in a corporate setting and still feel called to drive an organization forward. I sense this is probably an interim assignment and not something I'll do for a decade. Yet I've embraced this as a season where I can work to develop a habit of bravery.

Life is really a series of risks. Should you marry this person or wait on another? Either is risky. Should you take the job at the flashy new start-up company or keep climbing the ladder where you are? Both involve taking a risk. You know life is risky if you've ever moved away to attend college or made a financial investment or purchased a house or dropped your child off at kindergarten. The best leaders learn to think clearly and quickly and determine which risks are worth taking. But despite the propensity to take regular, calculated risks throughout their lives, many leaders find it difficult, almost impossible, to take them in their professional lives.

The biggest hurdle to developing a habit of bravery is fear. Nothing will paralyze you, hold you down, or push you forward in the wrong direction like this emotion. But sometimes the best way to cure a fear is to stare it squarely in the face.

Lots of things frighten me. Bees, wasps, spiders, and even pit bulls, mainly because I was bitten by one when I was just six. But growing up in Oklahoma, nothing put a fear into me like storms. Actually, that's a bit of an understatement. I had astraphobia, or an acute fear of storms. When clouds darkened and thunder clapped, tears would well up in my eyes and my knees would turn to Jell-O. If I woke and saw a tempest outside my bedroom window, I would feign being sick so I wouldn't have to leave the house. If my eye caught a flash of lightning, I would run to the principal's office. I was absolutely petrified of storms—scared out of my mind.

> 🐦 **SOMETIMES THE BEST WAY TO CURE A FEAR IS TO STARE IT SQUARELY IN THE FACE.**

One day, a storm was brewing outside, and anxiety crept up inside of me. I knew I could continue to run and hide or face it down. When the first drops of rain fell, I walked toward the door. Turning the handle and flinging it open, I now stood face-to-face with my worst fear. Mustering every drop of courage I possessed, I stepped outside and made myself stand underneath the weeping clouds. It was horrific and liberating. Soon my panic dissipated, and I began to breathe easy.

Over time, jumping into teenage years, I grew more comfortable during downpours, and storms soon became one of my greatest interests. I developed a love for them, and in college I even considered majoring in meteorology. Facing my fear not only became the portal to conquering it, but it increased my capacity for other kinds of bravery.

When the paperwork for my new consulting company arrived in the mail, I thought back to the day I'd stared down the deluge. By striking out on my own, I was facing a storm of sorts. Because I had beaten the storm before, I was more confident I could handle it this time around.

Every leader faces a unique set of storms over the course of his or her career. If you're not in the midst of a downpour now, you probably just came out of one or are about to encounter one. The difference maker in these moments is bravery.

- Bravery is the ability to do something that frightens you.
- Bravery is not the absence of fear but rather the commitment to face fear head-on, control it, and eventually, overcome it.
- Bravery is the willingness to "push the button" after you've counted the costs and know it is the right thing to do.
- Bravery is what gives you the confidence to conquer your innermost anxieties, to resist the impulse to shy away from the things that make you afraid.
- Bravery is the force that battles against your impulse to resist risk.
- Bravery is not only energy exerted in an extraordinary moment, but a lifelong habit the best leaders pursue.

Fear is the calling crippler. Bravery is the antidote. Sadly, while most influencers I meet *desire* to be courageous, most aren't. This may be due to the evasive nature of courage.

Think about the leaders you admire, and I'm sure bravery is a characteristic they each have. Leaders often idolize heroes like Winston Churchill, Nelson Mandela, Abraham Lincoln, Martin Luther King Jr., and Susan B. Anthony. These figures had guts and pluck. We tell stories about brave people scaling mountains or surviving natural disasters or escaping the throes of death. But how does one even begin to emulate their examples, in both his personal and professional lives?

Life begins at the end of your comfort zone. Choose courage over comfort. Today you may just need to step out and step up and step in and step over. Ralph Waldo Emerson said it this way: "What we fear doing most is usually what we most need to do."

Everyday leaders stepping out and taking a risk will never know what kind of ripple effect that creates. Martin Luther King lived this out. And all of us need people to help us be courageous. Even during MLK's most famous speech, "I Have a Dream," he needed help. The speech was actually not his prepared talk. But a friend continually yelled from the side of the stage, "Tell 'em about the dream, Martin!" He needed someone else to propel his courage forward.

Courage can seem elusive and beyond one's reach. But over the years, I've noticed that courage can be cultivated through practical steps that build into a habit of bravery:

- **TAKE SMALL STEPS; THEY LEAD TO BRAVE BOUNDS.** The best time to learn how to be courageous is not the moment you need to access courage. Leaders have to build up their reserves of bravery. Bravery is the rocket fuel for vision and a clear sense of calling and assignment to come alive. Eleanor Roosevelt said, "Do one thing every day that scares you." This seems like good advice to me. What we need is everyday bravery, not the kind of thing that makes headlines or that bards write songs about. Take time to build courage over time by taking risks in everyday and ordinary matters.

- **EMBRACE UNCERTAINTY.** As a leader, uncertainty is part of your job description. If it weren't, your company could replace you with a robot or an algorithm. So wherever there is uncertainty, there will always be a need for leaders. When the wind changes direction, don't recoil. Lunge forward instead. Practice bringing calm to chaos, clarity to the unknown, and confidence to uncertain circumstances.

- **BECOME A COST CALCULATOR.** Learn to calculate the pros and cons, costs and benefits, positives and negatives, upsides and downsides. Practice this in the small decisions. You're not trying to re-create the Wild West. You want to learn to take *calculated* risks. Of course, bravery sometimes means making a decision when the cons outweighs the pros, but if you become a cost calculator, at least you'll know what you're getting into ahead of time.

> 🐦 **PRACTICE BRINGING CALM TO CHAOS, CLARITY TO THE UNKNOWN, AND CONFIDENCE TO UNCERTAIN CIRCUMSTANCES.**

- **DELEGATE, ALREADY.** Leaders are often tempted to pass off responsibility while holding on to authority. But liberally delegating is one of the most courageous things you can do. Learn to relinquish control. If you want your team to be courageous, give them the chance to lead early and often. Pass on responsibilty and authority.

- **ENCOURAGE, DON'T DISCOURAGE.** Nothing will make your team skittish faster than discouraging their attempts to take risks or failing to recognize when their attempts pay off. Give your people the power, permission, and invitation to be brave by affirming them in their work. As a leader, you are in the business of making people confident. And confidence is a necessary ingredient for courage. Words can either be life giving or soul shattering. Choose the former. Give courage; don't steal it.
- **KEEP RISKING.** Age and success can make you way too comfortable. Stick with it. Don't lose your ability to take risks. Keep stepping out the older you get. Don't build a nest of complacency and laziness. The more one has, the fewer risks one will take. Fear can be a speed bump, but it should never be a stop sign.

As you integrate these practices into your life and work, a question will loom large: *What if I take a risk and lose?* I'm sorry to tell you, but you won't win every hand you play. Not every story you tell will have a happy ending. Sometimes you will crunch all the numbers and feel you are making the safest bet imaginable, but you'll roll the dice and lose your shirt.

Failure. Is. Not. The. End. Of. The. World.

In fact, failure is necessary and good. It will teach you how to make better decisions in the future and take anxiety out of your everyday decisions. Those who've failed much don't fear failure like those who've only tasted success. Don't let failure hold you back, as failure signals you're actually in the game and not sitting on the sidelines, complaining but not doing anything. Trying and failing is better than never trying and never failing. I would rather fail at pursuing my calling with courage and passion than succeed at something that doesn't really matter. Your greatest adversity may also be your greatest opportunity.

Before I left Catalyst, I'd begun work on an event in London. This was quite a risk, as it was the first time we'd attempted to launch an event outside of the United States. We had some key partners lined up and a possible venue, but we didn't know how we were going to pull it off.

> 🐦 **THOSE WHO'VE FAILED MUCH DON'T FEAR FAILURE LIKE THOSE WHO'VE ONLY TASTED SUCCESS.**

After visiting the city, dialoguing with friends there, and researching the possibility, I decided it was the right time. This was a risk, but not a blind one. We set up a web page, began recruiting a UK leadership team, and started talking about it externally.

That was a couple of years ago now, and Catalyst has still never hosted an event outside of the United States. It didn't work out. We weren't ready for it and had to pull back. And you know what? That's okay. Our team learned a lot that will come in handy if they decide to revisit it in the future.

Sometimes you face down the storm and conquer it. These experiences are exhilarating. Other times, you'll stand in the midst of the lightning storm and realize you're in danger and should retreat back indoors. These experiences can be crushing. Both require mettle, and both are necessary to developing a habit of bravery.

What would you pursue today if you weren't afraid to fail? If you knew for certain that you were the one to make it happen?

Go do that.

I challenge you to live a courageous life and lead in a courageous manner that someone would want to take notes on. Your decision to do something brave today may result in something greater than you ever imagined. Step out. Making a difference many times is just the simple courage to make a move. One move.

Courage is not a foolproof success generator. It is a virtue that opens up portals of possibility. Sometimes it will lead to success beyond your wildest imagination, and other times it will bring crippling (but constructive) defeat. Both will make you a stronger leader. So go be brave.

JULIA IMMONEN ON BRAVERY

JULIA IMMONEN IS THE AUTHOR OF ROW FOR FREEDOM AND
FOUNDER OF SPORT FOR FREEDOM.

You want to be more brave? Set some new physical challenges that push you to your limits. Since I'm a fitness and adventure freak, this works well for me. But I think it is just good advice in general. It's amazing how physical activity pushes and stretches our mental capacity. You feel like you can do anything after a dynamic workout, hike, or challenging bike ride.

Having great mentors who believe in you is crucial. Their encouragement keeps me going. Remain passionate and maintain a proper perspective! It's passion that causes me to keep taking risks. Most of my journey has felt like constant leaps of faith, doing things I'm fearful of. I hated public speaking at first, but remembering the bigger cause of millions who need me to be a voice for the voiceless gave me courage to stand up and share my voice. I just choose to do it afraid.

SCOTT HARRISON ON BRAVERY

SCOTT HARRISON IS FOUNDER OF CHARITY: WATER.

For me, courage has meant trying to fix broken things I see in the world by creating new business practices and approaches that most of the time don't fit neatly into the status quo. The key has been radical and frequent experimentation where I pursue creative ideas and then measure the results. This has also meant having hard conversations. One of my biggest personal challenges has been my aversion to conflict. I'm a peacemaker, and naturally just want everyone to get along. I've worked hard to run *toward* conflict, have hard conversations, and deal with tense issues in a timely manner.

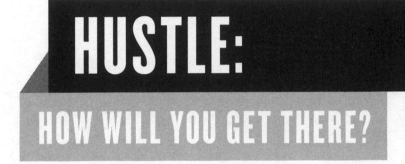

HUSTLE:

HOW WILL YOU GET THERE?

THIRTEEN

A HABIT OF EXCELLENCE

SET STANDARDS THAT SCARE YOU

When an organization hires me as a consultant to evaluate their personnel, policies, and practices, I often feel they expect me to act like a business school professor. After a full review, they wait expectantly to hear my feedback and expect a detailed explanation of how they should restructure their organizational chart or a bold, ten-year plan to triple annual revenue. More than one customer has been surprised when my primary advice consists of only three words: "Stop being average."

I agree with Martin Luther King Jr., who once said, "If a man is called to be a street sweeper, he should sweep streets even as a Michelangelo painted . . . that all the hosts of heaven and earth will pause to say, 'Here lived a great street sweeper who did his job well."

Establishing a habit of excellence begins with a core commitment to set a standard that scares the daylights out of you. Some people think excellence means being as good as the next guy. These leaders will take a product or philosophy from someone successful and replicate it. This happens often with pastors who are just trying to be as good a communicator as the preacher down the street. It happens a lot with salespeople who strive to have better numbers than the person in the cubicle next to them.

Greatness is not a destination. It's a journey. You never arrive at greatness. The goal is to set a standard that scares you to death and then continue trying to raise that standard.

But scary standards aren't weighed against the nearest competitor. They are derived from what the best of the best might look like in your context and calling. If you're coaching the Baltimore Ravens, for example, you don't want to be as good as the New York Giants. Your standard is to win the Super Bowl.

As Nick Saban, the famed coach of Alabama, who has won three national championships in the last five years, stated, "We aren't competing against an opponent necessarily. We're competing against perfection." So set a standard that scares you.

Being the best and pursuing excellence isn't about being big or having the largest budget or costly expense accounts. Excellence is ultimately about effort. For Hall of Fame basketball coach John Wooden, success wasn't just winning; it was the pursuit of the best. Achieving a standard was how Wooden measured success. The quality of his team's effort to realize their potential counted first and foremost. Coach Wooden was more upset with not playing up to the team's potential in a win versus playing as well as they could before a loss.

I also saw this growing up with our Bristow High School football team. Since my dad was one of the coaches, I had an inside track on seeing the pursuit of excellence. Basically, no budget was available, yet a standard of excellence was constant. They watched what college teams were doing and learned from the best, all the while realizing an average dressing room and broken-down weight machine was reality. My dad and the coaching staff didn't have any bells and whistles, but the one thing we could do like the great college teams was hustle. They conducted practices with army-like precision. Every drill was done to perfection. Sprints were run, and run a lot. Hustle from one part of practice to the next during two a days in one-hundred-degree Oklahoma heat was required. Our mind-set was greatness. And it showed. From 1975 to 1995, Bristow was one of the winningest programs in the state of Oklahoma.

Excellence is what helps a leader and an organization move from competent to exceptional, from good enough to soaring heights. What are the barely attainable standards you can turn into benchmarks? How can you begin pointing to the farthest points on the horizon and then motivating you and your team to race there? These are the practices that will make your organization unusual and force your average competitors to begin mimicking you rather than the other way around.

> 🐦 **SCARY STANDARDS AREN'T WEIGHED AGAINST THE NEAREST COMPETITOR. THEY ARE DERIVED FROM WHAT THE BEST OF THE BEST MIGHT LOOK LIKE IN YOUR CONTEXT AND CALLING.**

Once a client gets over the initial shock of my blunt advice, they follow up with a comment and a question: *"We didn't know we were mediocre."* and *"How can we stop being average?"* The answer to their query depends largely on the organization and where they find themselves, but many principles are universal.

Author and screenwriter Neil Gaiman, in a 2012 commencement address at the University of the Arts, said that excellence in business can be boiled down to three simple things:

1. Be Efficient: Turn in work on time.
2. Be Effective: Do great work.
3. Be Congenial: Be a pleasure to work with.[1]

Gaiman added that even mastering two of the three will take you far. If you do great work and are a pleasure to work with, most people will forgive you for missing a deadline. If you're always on time and a pleasure to work with, most people put up with less than perfect work. If you turn in great work on time, most people will put up with you being unpleasant.

Pixar has become known as the gold standard of filmmaking in Hollywood. But their films aren't great from the beginning. They describe them early on as their "ugly babies," but everyone wants to make sure they turn out great. And no one wants to be the first producer or director to have a film that stinks. Their culture of excellence has demanded habits of excellence. According to Ed Catmull, a cofounder of Pixar, "The first version is not perfect, but we have to keep making it better because the standard of greatness at Pixar creates a mindset that no one wants to let anyone else down."[2] For the last twenty years, every Pixar film has opened number one at the box office opening weekend.

It's difficult to argue with Gaiman's analysis, which makes for a good starting point as you develop this habit. But excellence is also more practical. It's the small actions in the everyday that help focus us on scary standards. Here are some principles I often give people that can help take your organization and leadership potential from average to exceptional.

- **REMEMBER PEOPLE'S NAMES . . . FOR "PETE'S" SAKE AND YOURS.** Whether you are dealing with clients or meeting with colleagues, always remember and address them by their names. In a moment when people are often viewed as job titles or potential sales, this will make a massive difference in your work.

- **LOOK INTO EYEBALLS, NOT OVER SHOULDERS.** Nothing annoys me more than talking to someone whose mind is somewhere else. If you're scanning a room or checking your smartphone, it sends a clear message to the person you're speaking with: you'd prefer to be somewhere else. It doesn't matter if you're chatting about the weekend with a coworker at the water cooler or chatting with a donor at the buffet table in a banquet hall; always look people in the eye.

- **LEARN TO ANTICIPATE.** Excellence requires always being one step ahead. This is intentional and requires a constant answering of "What should I prepare for that I haven't experienced but will?" Do something every day that you weren't asked or told to do. And brainstorm with your team about what tomorrow will (likely) bring. This is true regarless of your role, title, or position. Leading from wherever you are means intentionally making decisions like you are in charge, most often without the perceived authority.

> 🐦 **THE BEST IDEAS COME OUT OF THE KILN OF DISAGREEMENT AND DISCERNMENT.**

- **EMBRACE PUSHBACK.** The best ideas come out of the kiln of disagreement and discernment. Almost every successful leader I know wants their team members to challenge the process, question assumptions, bring new ideas to the table, and push back when they don't agree. Don't be afraid to do this. If you are unsure about whether you have "permission" from those above you to push back, ask for permission on the front end of meetings. If your leader is not mature enough to take this, that's a problem.

- **DEMAND FEEDBACK.** Use every opportunity to improve. Whether it's a presentation, negotiation, meeting with clients, or sales call, ask those around you how you can get better. Recently I was speaking in Atlanta at a staff retreat for a friend's organization. A few of the Catalyst team were there with me, and I asked them what could be better about my talk. I wanted to hear what could improve, not what they thought was great. But I had to demand they give me a list of things I did poorly because their natural inclination was to tell me the things I did right.

- **COME TO MEETINGS WITH SOLUTIONS, NOT JUST IDEAS.** Ideas are great—they are the lifeblood of a habit of innovation, after all—but ideas must always lead somewhere. Do you have a finish line? Do you know what a win would look like when it comes to your ideas? Always move toward completion and not away from it. If your ideas don't solve a problem, improve a process, or create organizational energy, they might as well never have existed.

- **TAKE ON MORE RESPONSIBILITY.** Ask for more involvement, and you'll be lifting the load off your employer or boss. It's always a welcomed conversation. Help by taking on more.

- **CONSTANTLY IMPROVE.** Great leaders and teams guard against complacency and acceptance of the status quo. Though you should always celebrate successes and goal achievements, these are also opportunities for you to set your sights even higher. Don't allow mediocrity to set in. Push yourself daily, and create shared accountability for improvement across the entire team.

- **REWARD EXCELLENCE WITH CULTURE.** If you don't create a culture of excellence, your team won't have excellent ideas and create excellent products. On the front end of projects, set expectations of which goals must be achieved and which standards cannot be compromised. On the back end, find ways to pass on perks to your key team members who've gone the extra mile. Whether it's tickets to an NFL game, a free golf outing, books, Moleskine notebooks, or a day off, show your appreciation by a few extra gifts here and there. And make sure to surround yourself with people who are way better than you at their role. Go and find the best. If you are the smartest person in every office in your organization, that's a problem.

- **CREATE CONSISTENCY.** Excellent leaders who are great at what they do create excellent teams. Excellent teams then create excellent results. Excellence is about consistency. Remarkability is built from the continual steadfast pursuit of being the best. It's not about lots of money or a huge staff. It's a mind-set and a standard. If making copies, be the best copy maker ever. If mixing up a mocha at Starbucks, be the best barista in that city. If negotiating a new contract, be the best negotiator in the company. If planning a conference, put on the best conference in your entire industry. Set your standards so high that it may seem impossible to reach them, and stick to it. Be a yardstick by which all others measure their mediocrity. Jonathan Ive, the famed designer at Apple, says, "It's very easy to be different, but very difficult to be better."

Resist the temptation to dismiss all this excellence talk as the idolatry of success or perfectionism run amok. This habit is actually deeply connected to our spirituality.

The Bible says that the prophet Daniel was "distinguished above all the other high officials and satraps, because an excellent spirit was in him" (Daniel 6:3 ESV; cf. 5:12). Proverbs 22:29 opines, "Do you see a man skillful in his work? He will stand before kings; he will not stand before obscure men" (ESV). And Ecclesiastes 9:10 exhorts workers to be excellent: "Whatever your hand finds to do, do it with all your might."

The quality of work we do is not just about bragging rights. It's about stewardship. We serve a great God who doesn't settle for average. God has created the world (and you) with excellence and purpose, and God has buried gifts inside of you that can create excellent products and build excellent organizations. Committing to a habit of excellence just means doing great things with the tools God has entrusted to you.

> **THE QUALITY OF WORK WE DO IS NOT JUST ABOUT BRAGGING RIGHTS. IT'S ABOUT STEWARDSHIP.**

Serving God should elevate our level of excellence in every part of our lives, not lower it. Don't wait on a company handbook or your boss to provide you with a standard of excellence. Allow your faith to be the standard that pushes you to greatness. Choose to be so great that people can't ignore you.

Want credibility in culture? Then be great. Culture is attracted to things done well. A habit of excellence gives me credibility for building a bridge and winning the right to be heard. Love people by being great and create credibility through assignments done well.

Centuries later, the apostle Paul echoes and modifies the Old Testament teachings on excellence by saying, "So whether you eat or drink or whatever you do, do it all for the glory of God" (1 Corinthians 10:31).

Glorify God by being the greatest leader, parent, neighbor, classmate, friend, and employee.

The glory of God?

Talk about a scary standard.

PERRY NOBLE ON EXCELLENCE

PERRY NOBLE IS PASTOR OF NEWSPRING CHURCH IN ANDERSON, SOUTH CAROLINA.

Excellence is not perfection; it's simply giving God your very best. Leaders need to know the difference between excellence and extravagance. Extravagance means spending more money than necessary, and covering up the problems that are already there. If your team keeps saying, "Things would be better *if* we had this or that" then take notice. This is a warning sign. When people start promising to do more when they have more, then they have excused extravagance with excellence.

Rather than investing more money, excellence means investing more time, and often on the small things. Excellence is showing up early and double-checking to make sure things are done well. Excellence is starting and ending on time. Excellence is making sure the bathrooms are clean. These are "small things" but excellence requires that they get done.

Excellence is the result of hard work and paying attention to details.

JEREMY COWART ON EXCELLENCE

JEREMY COWART IS AN AWARD-WINNING DESIGNER, ARTIST, AND PHOTOGRAPHER, AND FOUNDER OF HOPE: PORTRAIT.

I'm at my best when I start with exercise. Exercise sets the tone for how I treat myself the rest of the day. My stress levels are far lower when I keep my inbox empty. I get overwhelmed if I have fifty to one hundred e-mails sitting in my inbox that require my attention. So less inbox clutter allows me to think clearer. I'm an Evernote junkie so every thought or idea I have immediately gets dumped into Evernote. I love keeping ideas organized and searchable. I also use Nozbe to keep me on schedule.

Putting teams together helps me lead better and pursue excellence. I'm an idea guy, so as soon as I have an idea to pursue, the first step is to find the right people who have the strengths to balance my weaknesses. Ideas matter. Occasionally shut off all your digital devices and just do a free-form brainstorming and write down any and every idea you can think up and dream to pursue later.

FOUR TIPS ON EXCELLENCE FROM JON ACUFF

JON ACUFF IS THE BESTSELLING AUTHOR OF *DO OVER*, *QUITTER*, AND *START*.

- **[STICK] WITH SOMETHING.** I've been writing the same concept blog for a number of years. There are seasons when I want to write and other times I don't. Sticking with it allows me to improve.
- **MAKE IT PUBLIC.** I love having lots of folks challenging me, and taking something public is a way to get feedback.
- **KEEP PEOPLE AROUND YOU WHO ENCOURAGE YOU TO HUSTLE.** Surround yourself with people who will challenge you when you're pushing too hard or too easy.
- **TRACKING IT IS IMPORTANT.** With the last book I wrote, I knew it would be a harder process. So I tracked the process. I wrote a number of hours I wanted to work on it and made sure to track the number and my progress.

FOURTEEN

A HABIT OF STICK-WITH-IT-NESS

TAKE THE LONG VIEW

One day toward the end of my sabbatical, I decided to call and talk to my parents. As often happens during conversations with one's parents, we began reminiscing. The antics, the mistakes, the victories of childhood and adolescence.

"Do you remember the time in high school when I ran a mile in just over five minutes so I could make the football team?" I asked.

"Of course. But you didn't just wake up one morning and decide to do it," my dad replied, "Almost every day for weeks before try-outs, you worked at it, building up your speed and stamina. You started with a handful of laps, moved to a half mile, and then honed the full mile. Those who didn't train like you, probably didn't make the team."

Playing football for Bristow High School was an honor. To make the team, each player had to run a mile in a certain time, depending on your playing position. This meant you had to work out and run during the summer to make sure you could finish in that time. It wasn't about the time necessarily. It was more about putting practices and a habit in place during the summer to make sure you were running and staying in shape, so once football season started in August, the coach wasn't dealing with a bunch of out-of-shape bozos—but instead we were ready to go.

When we hung up that day, I spent the afternoon internalizing what my dad had said. His memory was correct. I vividly remember all the early mornings I crawled out of bed against my will and strapped on my running shoes. The pain of early evening sprint cramps had somehow drifted out of my mind, but now the memories were rushing back. The entire summer before football tryouts was a grueling time of training for that test, requiring me to keep my eyes on what I wanted to achieve many months away.

Those who failed to take the long view and procrastinated—just as my dad surmised—ended up having to run every day after two-a-day practices to try and make the team. Running until they made their required time. Needless to say, not fun!

When I consider my life, all the moments that might be loosely labeled "success" were prepared for. They were fought for. They were the product of many days and months, sometimes years, of planning and organization and preparation. These were not creations of happenstance but products of having persevered over the long haul.

And such is life.

The information age has made this habit increasingly difficult because the most sensational stories rise to the top. We're inundated with instant and uncommon success stories. It's easy to believe the exception is the rule. We forget that the vast majority of thriving leaders arrived at their current positions through years of toil and sacrifice. Their platforms and credibility were constructed with the mortar of patience. We fail to remember that most profitable business ventures took years—decades, perhaps—of effort, involving many people.

Similarly, the innovation age has made this habit less common because the modern tendency is to assume that "newer" always means "better." Whenever we hear about a new process or product, we want to pitch our old one and attain the newer, "better" one. But this behavior is not actually innovation; it is impulsiveness. True creativity is discerning, and it balances the need for "new" with patience and perseverance.

Instead of letting the influences of the information and innovation age throw us out of whack, leaders must instead learn to be disciplined:

DISCIPLINED IN THE NOW: We all want to grow and progress, but leaders must learn to be faithful to what is front of them. Even if you're looking frantically for another job, stay focused and engaged in your current role. The way you behave in the "now" is practice for the "later."

DISCIPLINED IN THE LITTLE: God doesn't judge based on what we do, but based on what we do with what we have. It doesn't matter if you are the lowest name on the organizational chart and responsible for stewarding only a nickel of budget money. Turning a nickel into a dime is just as significant as turning one million dollars into two. As Luke 16:10 says, "He who is faithful in a very little thing is faithful also in much; and he who is unrighteous in a very little thing is unrighteous also in much" (NASB). Prove yourself worthy with the little.

DISCIPLINED IN THE IMPORTANT: Spend most of your time worrying about the most important things. Don't become so rigorously committed to your job duties that you forsake your family or friends or faith. That isn't discipline; it's dereliction.

Learning to stick with it transforms "microwave leaders" into "Crock-Pot leaders." Crock-Pot leaders—not to be confused with crackpot leaders—have learned to take the long view and see beyond the momentary. They resist the temptation to abandon a perfectly seaworthy ship whenever they lose interest or grow stir-crazy. They develop rigorous disciplines in their everyday lives that help keep them on task and progressing.

> 🐦 **DON'T BECOME SO RIGOROUSLY COMMITTED TO YOUR JOB DUTIES THAT YOU FORSAKE YOUR FAMILY OR FRIENDS OR FAITH. THAT ISN'T DISCIPLINE; IT'S DERELICTION.**

Discipline is difficult, but especially for young leaders today. We find sticking with something for longer than five minutes tough. But perseverance and diligence are crucial. Long obedience in the same direction, as Eugene Peterson says. This is true in friendships as well. Maintaining a friendship with someone for more than ten years is harder today than ever.

My friend Robert Madu says it this way: In a culture where quitting is normal, be crazy enough to stay committed, foolish enough to be faithful, and stupid enough to stick with it! Steady Eddy always beats Sexy Steve.

Many leaders who quit the work they are doing after experiencing failure, growing bored, or getting discouraged may have been only moments from breaking through and finding success. So learn to settle in, stay faithful, and stick with it.

That's the *what* and *why* of stick-with-it-ness. The *how* is far more difficult.

Bobby Knight, the one-time winningest coach in men's college basketball, once said, "It has always been my thought that the most important single ingredient to success in athletics or life is discipline.

I have many times felt that this word is the most ill-defined in all of our language. My definition of the word is as follows: 1. Do what has to be done; 2. When it has to be done; 3. As well as it can be done; and 4. Do it that way all the time."[1]

Stick-with-it-ness is the foundation for legacy. And legacy starts now, wherever you are in life. As Bob Foster used to tell me constantly while working at Lost Valley Ranch, "Brad, your twenties establish your seventies. The man of God you want to become when you're seventy-five is the man of God you're becoming when you're twenty-five." The way you start determines how you finish.

Track stars understand the importance of starting well. Coming out of "the clips" in the start of the race is vital to finishing in first place. Marine boaters knows this—if you're off by just a tiny amount in the beginning of the ocean journey, you'll end up hundreds of miles from your destination days or weeks later. A slightly off-course start will create a slow decline that can derail you in the long term.

Stay in your lane and take the long view. Do you want to be a mushroom or an oak tree? A mushroom takes six days to mature, while an oak tree takes sixty years. God can give you favor instantly, but I believe true influence is gained over time, through the process. Herschel Walker, former Heisman Trophy winner and famed college and NFL running back, says, "My God-given talent is my ability to stick with something longer than anyone else."

Here are a few of the most practical tips for stick-with-it-ness that have worked for me and leaders I respect.

- **REGIMENT YOUR DAY.** How much of each day are your spending with family? On work? With your spouse? In prayer? If you don't manage your schedule, it will become impossible to manage. Instead, work on regimenting the day and keeping a scorecard of how long and when you perform certain tasks.

Begin with the areas where you don't need regimentation. For example, begin brushing your teeth each morning at 7:12 a.m. for two unbroken minutes. Not because it is right or holy but because you're working to strengthen a muscle. Along the way, identify your weaknesses. Are you usually late? Are you on time but inconsistent? Do you tend to quit midway through? This will help you learn how to develop disciplines.

- **REMOVE TEMPTATIONS.** I've never understood why people who are trying to lose weight keep their pantry stocked with junk food or why those who struggle with pornography addiction refuse to install protective software on their personal computers. If you find yourself struggling to commit to the most important disciplines in your life, gather up the bad influences and toss them out with the trash.

- **CRASH THROUGH YOUR QUITTING POINTS.** Every runner knows that the peak of pain precedes a rush of adrenaline and endorphins. When you feel as though you need to quit, commit to another minute, hour, day of time. Crashing through your quitting points is a great way to build stamina over time.

- **DON'T BE A DICTATOR.** The goal of stick-with-it-ness is to keep you moving forward, not to remove all variations from your life. If you're on a diet, treat yourself to a piece of pie on occasion. If you're regimenting your time, schedule regular breaks. Are you reining in your spending? Reward yourself with a little fun money at the end of the month to use for entertainment or recreation. Unbending disciplines often lead to self-loathing, but flexible discipline will lead to self-control.

- **HAVE DOUBLE GOALS.** Every leader should be working toward daily goals and legacy goals. The actions that move you and your organization forward on a regular basis are daily goals. These will often be standing benchmarks and recurrent. Arriving at the office at a certain time, sending handwritten notes, encouraging team members, and achieving high sales numbers fall under this category. Legacy goals look at the future—the end points and the high points. This could be writing a book, winning an award, being able to retire, or—if you're a professional football player with a career span of a few years or less—winning a Super Bowl.

See yourself as a steward. Have an ownership mentality. Be phenomenal in the middle of wherever you are. My time at Lost Valley Ranch in Colorado clearly taught me this lesson. With 150 horses, stewarding each steed like your own child was a bit of a challenge. No guest wanted to climb aboard a dirty horse with a dirty, worn-out saddle. Plus, horses tend to poop. And poop a lot. So being a pooper scooper became one of my main responsibilities. My posture was always to scoop manure as if it were the most important assignment I'd ever received. Be faithful with where you are and what you've been given.

> 🐦 **UNBENDING DISCIPLINES OFTEN LEAD TO SELF-LOATHING, BUT FLEXIBLE DISCIPLINE WILL LEAD TO SELF-CONTROL.**

His name is Tychicus, and you've probably never heard of him. His name appears in the sixth chapter of the biblical book of Ephesians, and when we encounter him here, Tychicus is in something of a bind. He's in prison, which in the first century didn't come with cable TV, three meals a day, or daily recreational time. This was a brutal existence that often involved physical abuse, malnutrition, maddening boredom, and uncertainty about one's future.

But Tychicus isn't alone in prison. He's there with his friend, the apostle Paul. In fact, he's in prison *because* he had been ministering with Paul and wanted to stay with his friend to the bitter end. I don't know if there is anyone or anything I'm committed to stick with if it means prison time, but that person was Paul and that thing was the gospel for Tychicus. As a result, Paul calls him "dear brother and faithful servant in the Lord" (Ephesians 6:21).

Whenever I flounder in life and am tempted to hit the eject button, I always think of that oddly named saint. You may never name your son after him, but he has been immortalized in the pages of the Bible because he possessed one single virtue: stick-with-it-ness. He was faithful in the now, the little, and the important. And he was faithful to the end.

So commit today to establishing the necessary disciplines you need to push ahead where you've been planted. Commit to the nitty-gritty, to the daily grind, to the small and big. Keep walking steadfastly in the mundane, knowing that our faithfulness in the ordinary often leads to the extraordinary. Don't trade away a lifelong promise from God to satisfy a short-term appetite. And even when you don't feel like getting up and running that mile, remember that one day you'll reminisce about how that ordinary commitment contributed to who you have become and what you have achieved.

CARLOS WHITTAKER ON STICK-WITH-IT-NESS

CARLOS WHITTAKER IS A BLOGGER, SPEAKER, WORSHIP LEADER, AND AUTHOR OF *MOMENT MAKER*.

I used to either live "in the clouds" or "on the ground." The truth is, the hardest part of leadership is the taking off and the landing. Let me get specific with three things:

- I wake up at 5 a.m. to exercise and begin working at 6 a.m. I get more done by the time most people walk into work than they will probably accomplish all day.
- I don't open my e-mail until 9 a.m. E-mail gives the steering wheel of my car to someone else. When I open it, I am no longer in charge. So I wait until after I'm finished with *me* to help *them*.
- The runway for me is my family. So when I land the plane and walk in the door to my home, there is a box. The box is called the "freedom box." All of our digital devices go into this box until everyone goes to bed. I am laser focused when the phone is in the box.

RYAN O'NEAL ON STICK-WITH-IT-NESS

RYAN O'NEAL IS AN AWARD-WINNING ARTIST WHO PRODUCES MUSIC UNDER THE NAME "SLEEPING AT LAST."

To-do lists are a matter of sanity and insanity for me. Without them, everything feels impossible. Not to mention, the aftermath of a checked-off to-do list is that warm and fuzzy feeling of productivity.

One item that is always on my to-do list is "write." In Julia Cameron's *The Artist Way*, she details the concept and value of "morning pages." This is the practice of waking up and writing three pages (give or take) each day, whether or not you feel like you have anything to say. The idea is that by writing each day, nonsense or otherwise, you empty your cache and start your day with clarity. Creative or not, I believe the practice of writing every day will have a great effect on the fluidity of your work and the strength of your leadership.

JEFF SHINABARGER ON STICK-WITH-IT-NESS

JEFF SHINABARGER IS FOUNDER OF PLYWOOD PEOPLE AND AUTHOR OF *MORE OR LESS.*

Part of discipline for me is when I wake up. I get up at 5:45 in the morning. I have heard many times that the most successful people in the world are awake before 6 a.m. I don't know if that is true, but I know that I have the ability to get the greatest amount of self-leadership done prior to seven o'clock in the morning. This is the time I work out, read, pray, and write. I don't do all of these every day, but I do some of them every day. That is the time to focus on me, God, and what is most important to further my calling.

FIFTEEN

A HABIT OF EXECUTION

COMMIT TO COMPLETION

My drenched hands worked furiously as thunder clapped overhead. When I began repairing the corral fence an hour earlier, the sky was a palette of blue. But forty minutes into the project, clouds rolled in and showered down on my team and me. We pressed on with our work.

Now, a little rain never hurt anyone, but lightning is nothing to mess around with. Determined to finish the job, I ignored the dangers. I came to regret this decision moments later when the heavens grew angry and released their electric fury. Lightning struck the fence while my hand still gripped the barbwire.

After the flash of light, all I remember was waking up in a pile of manure, staring back at two horses who looked as confused as I. As the pace of my world sped up to normal, I began to pat my body and make sure all my limbs were still attached. They were. Luckily, I had been wearing gloves that day; otherwise I'd be writing this book in between harp lessons in the Great Beyond.

That story will always be seared—somewhat literally—in my memory for two reasons. First, it reminds me that one should always consider the safety and well-being of his or her team no matter the potential cost. But also, it is an emblem of a work ethic that was passed down to me from my father and has never left me. I'm a "get it done" kind of guy, and I hate failing to finish any project once I've started it.

Unfortunately, I've noticed that most of us are "middle of the pack" leaders. We don't want to work too much harder than others around us, because, heck, we won't necessarily make more money for it. And we don't want to work less than others around us, because, heck, we might get fired. So we slip into the middle of the pack, and work just hard enough to keep our jobs and fly under the radar. But we have to resist this temptation. Choose to outwork everyone else. Arrive early; stay late; do whatever it takes to produce a stellar product. Finish what you start, and complete the tasks we could easily put off. Great leaders are great finishers.

> **IT DOESN'T MATTER HOW MUCH OF A RACE YOU RUN IF YOU DON'T CROSS THE FINISH LINE. SIMILARLY, UNFINISHED PROJECTS MIGHT AS WELL NEVER HAVE BEEN STARTED.**

Henry Ford said it well: "You can't build a reputation on what you're going to do." When you're tempted to slack off or slow down, outwork everyone else. It doesn't matter how much of a race you run if you don't cross the finish line. Similarly, unfinished projects might as well never have been started. "However beautiful the strategy, you should occasionally look at the results," according to Winston Churchill.

That's why whenever I interviewed potential new team members over the years, I wanted to make sure that they were creative enough to generate ideas but also determined enough to see those ideas through to completion. One of the most valuable traits of any employee is his or her ability to execute and get things done. In fact,

I would suggest that in today's leadership climate, no other habit is more important than execution. Anyone can come up with a new idea, concept, or marketing plan. Ideas are overrated. What truly matters is whether you can take an idea from concept to completion. Whether you can carry the ball all the way down the field and cross the goal line. Everyone is required to execute and take projects from start to finish. It's a non-nonnegotiable in the new economy of leadership.

> "Effective leadership is not about making speeches or being liked;
> leadership is defined by results not attributes."
>
> —Peter Drucker

Though execution is a critical workplace skill, many leaders procrastinate before beginning, stall out once they've started, or give up before they've finished. Getting projects across the finish line, or what Seth Godin calls "shipping," is too often a rarity among leaders.

Why?

One reason is because strong leaders are often natural initiators. They are willing to take risks on fresh endeavors. They are energized by new projects, new divisions, new ideas. Launching into uncharted territory or tinkering with novel ideas gets their blood pumping. Initiation is a strength most great leaders share.

Because of this, some will hire and delegate the responsibility to execute to someone else. If you have the resources and means to take this step, it can often work—at least temporarily. But when there is a vacancy in that position, suddenly projects fall behind. And often the person in that position feels unsupported by the leader who isn't at all invested

> 🐦 **MANY LEADERS PROCRASTINATE BEFORE BEGINNING, STALL OUT ONCE THEY'VE STARTED, OR GIVE UP BEFORE THEY'VE FINISHED.**

> **SOME OF US NEED TO PUT DOWN THE MEGAPHONE AND JUST GRAB A SHOVEL. LITTLE LESS TALK, AND A LOT MORE ACTION.**

in the tasks that they must complete. So every leader must share the responsibility for getting the job done.

If you're an artist—a film director, graphic designer, or writer—this can be doubly difficult. Because creatives thrive on creativity, not processes. People-oriented leaders will also find this habit more challenging than task-oriented leaders, like myself. Those in these fields should be especially aware of their outstanding projects and intentional about making progress to execute. If you're a feeler or perceiver or creative, you will need to work harder at developing a habit of execution.

A few best practices that you might find helpful:

1. **CRAFT A PLAN AND CREATE ACCOUNTABILITY.** When an idea is generated, never leave the meeting without determining how the idea should move forward. If you kick the can down the road, you may never see it again. And even if one person is ultimately responsible for the project, assign coleaders to it as well. Delegating to multiple team members will create accountability and increase the project's chances of timely completion.

2. **FIGURE OUT YOUR GET-IT-DONE TIME OF DAY.** Notice when you are most productive, and lean into that. For me, it's the morning—I can get more done in the first three hours of the day than I can the entire rest of the day. So figure yours out and plan accordingly.

3. **REWARD COMPLETION AS MUCH AS YOU DO INITIATION.** Everyone wants credit for having an impactful idea and to be able to say, "I thought of that." But an organization thrives on all the support staff who drive the

idea forward. Make sure that everyone who works to complete the project is as rewarded and recognized as the one who had the flash of insight in the first place. Done is better than perfect.

4. **GET 'ER DONE.** Instead of an organization that defaults to "let's meet about it," build a culture that immediately thinks, *Let's make it happen.* A little less talk, and a lot more action, as the country song says. Fewer meetings, I believe, leads to more execution. If you must have a meeting, focus on solving a problem/creating a solution, not just informing people on what you could have e-mailed. Leaders are problem solvers, pure and simple. Be a problem solver and solution creator, instead of a problem creator and solution delayer.

5. **HIRE DOERS, NOT TALKERS.** Potential new hires will often brag about the projects they "oversee" at their current job. Make sure to dig deeper into what they actually *do* to execute on those projects. Scratch the surface and you'll often find their team deserves the lion's share of the credit for what they've "accomplished." Seek to hire hustlers. You're better off with an overzealous employee who even completes others' tasks without being asked than a daydreamer and brainstormer who must be motivated to execute. As mentioned earlier, it's easier to slow down a racehorse by having to pull back on the reins than to spur a field horse to get moving. As Will Rogers famously stated, "Even if you're on the right track, you'll get run over if you just sit there."

6. **LET YOUR TEAM MANAGE UP MORE THAN YOU MANAGE DOWN.** One of the goals of a leader is to help those who work under you to one day work beside you. This means reversing the micromanaging system that many type-A

leaders automatically set up so that you're executing while producing executors. Give away your managerial responsibilities to those who are normally the recipients of management and let them take tasks to completion.

7. **UNDERSTAND THAT ACTIONS SPEAK LOUD.** Let your actions speak way louder than your words. Your work serves as a mirror for your attitude, commitment, and service. Anticipate what your boss, client, or guests need before they ever ask for something. Be proactive by owning the relationship and the result. Your answer should never be "That's not my job." Take initiative to see the problem or issue through to the very end. Creating is hard work, so help create an action-leaning culture by working your guts out. Sweat equity is often the number one ingredient in success. Action creates traction, and impact comes from forward motion. Underwhelm with your words, but always overwhelm with your actions.

8. **MURDER, WHEN APPROPRIATE.** This habit must be handled with care. Don't complete a project for completion's sake. You'll often realize that an idea should be killed while you're still attempting to execute. When this becomes clear, murder it and move on. However, if you find dead bodies lying all over the floor, you should evaluate your creative process to determine why so many of the ideas your team is generating are unsustainable.

A habit of execution is one of the key differentiators between a leader and a manager because managers often wait on someone else to give them direction. They focus on maintaining the status quo among their team. They may motivate those under them, but they won't drive a new project forward unless their boss asks them to. Managers tend to want constant direction, so they make sure approval has been given and always cover their tracks in case something goes wrong. A manager will often feel content with a project remaining unfinished so long as it is not his responsibility or one of his team members isn't at fault.

Leaders, on the other hand, don't wait to be assigned a task. If they identify an undone task they can complete, they jump in. Their concern is for the organization at large rather than the performance of their direct reports. Execution energizes them.

So make sure you commit to completing projects in your organization no matter what . . . unless that means working outside in a lightning storm.

> 🐦 **YOU'LL OFTEN REALIZE THAT AN IDEA SHOULD BE KILLED WHILE YOU'RE STILL ATTEMPTING TO EXECUTE. WHEN THIS BECOMES CLEAR, MURDER IT AND MOVE ON.**

JEFF HENDERSON ON EXECUTION

JEFF HENDERSON IS PASTOR OF GWINNETT CHURCH, A CAMPUS OF NORTH POINT MINISTRIES.

If you don't execute, a dream is just a nap. Here are some actions I think are helpful to implement at the beginning of each week:

- Ask yourself, "What three key things do I have to get done this week?"
- Reflect on the past week, and *then* think about the next week.
- Write five handwritten notes to others.
- Review your weekly goals and get started.

The first and last one are especially important. I heard recently that only 3 percent of Americans have goals and only 1 percent of Americans write their goals down. If you are writing down your goals, then you are in the 99th percentile. The 1 percent of those who write down their goals will exponentially achieve more than the rest of the population.

PROPAGANDA ON EXECUTION

PROP IS A HIP-HOP ARTIST WITH HUMBLE BEAST RECORDS.

I learned about hard work from the idea of manual labor. I was raised by hardworking Latino men. These men laid concrete and built homes for a living. Almost every Saturday they would round up the boys and we would have to go to work with them and they would give us tasks and say, "You either do it right or do it twice. You are done when it's right." I hated it, but it changed the way I think about jobs. Execution means doing the job right the first time. Always leave a place or person better than you found it.

SIXTEEN

A HABIT OF TEAM BUILDING

CREATE AN ENVIRONMENT THAT ATTRACTS AND RETAINS THE BEST AND BRIGHTEST

When it comes to employee benefits, Silicon Valley is like Shangri-la. Forget 401(k)s, health insurance plans, and matched annuity contributions. That's child's-play, standard stuff. We're talking lavish stuff—free meals cooked by gourmet chefs, on-site gymnasiums, oil changes, even dry cleaning.

Having heard reports of these sorts of employee perks, I decided to spend some of my sabbatical in Silicon Valley, investigating it for myself. I visited the headquarters of famed organizations, such as Apple, Yahoo!, and Facebook. Each had its own unique touches intended to keep employees happy. Facebook's offices made me laugh a little because they felt like a fraternity house with writing all over the halls, Ping-Pong tables, and hordes of unshowered young people bouncing with energy. But no office impressed me more than Google's.

First, the physical space was stunning and thoughtfully laid out. Great lighting, open-air designs, appealing color palettes. Upon entering each sector of the sprawling campus, one can't help thinking, *I'd enjoy working in this space.* But the appeal for potential employees moves well beyond aesthetics.

The tech giant allows employees to bring their dogs to work, and they can give each other "massage credits" as a reward for professional accomplishments. They give new dads six weeks of paid time off, and new moms get eighteen weeks. They even offer these fresh parents "baby bonding bucks" to help pay for diapers, formula, and other necessities. The free gym offers fitness classes, and the organized intramural sports give employees a chance to exercise alongside their coworkers. Google provides their employees free rides to and from their Mountain View campus via Wi-Fi–enabled buses. From nap pods to help their workers rest to swimming pools to help their workers relax, Google HQ left me amazed.

> **WHEN YOU PRIORITIZE YOUR TEAM, YOUR TEAM WILL PRIORITIZE YOU.**

No wonder more than two million people apply to work at Google each year.

But such extravagant perks aren't about keeping up with the techie Joneses of Silicon Valley. They are also about creating an environment of unparalleled teamwork.

When commenting about how Google provides free breakfast, lunch, and dinner, one employee said, "It saves me time and money, and helps me build relationships with my colleagues."[1]

Google has mastered a principle the rest of us would do well to learn: when you prioritize your team, your team will prioritize you. How well do you treat your people? Do you honor them, appreciate them, find ways to make their lives better? Or do you only care about what they can do for you—to make you money or increase efficiency or perform a function? If you objectify others, they will reciprocate it.

Which analogy would you use to describe the way your organization views its employees? Are they numbers on a spreadsheet? Are they walking profit-and-loss algorithms? Are they gears in a machine?

A good analogy for your team might be a family. This doesn't mean that you'll always be warm and affectionate. What family doesn't have its share of dysfunction? You can expect to have a crazy uncle and a disgruntled sibling and an overinvolved parental figure. The diversity makes a family a family.

Or consider Pat Gelsinger, the first ever Chief Technology Officer at Intel and now CEO of VMware, who says he has learned to see his organization like a church: "At every phase of my career I've always said, 'Okay, now I'm in the next phase of my full-time ministry.' I like to think I have a congregation of 13,300 today as CEO of VMware. It's not Menlo Park Presbyterian Church or Reality Church. It's VMware, and that's the church that God has given me to be a minister to, and be a steward."

Pat added: "Leaders have incredible opportunity to impact lives. Projects come and go, companies rise and fall, people come and go, but impact on people lasts. If you worked with me at any point, you work with me forever. Build into people like they are on your team forever. You are always on my team. The magic of leadership is getting things done and bringing the team along with you on the way, and ultimately touching the lives of leaders."[2]

I like Gelsinger's advice, and it would certainly change the way most leaders look at their teams. A pastor knows that he depends on the congregation for his very livelihood, but leaders too often forget that the same is true of them.

Of course, most organizations don't have the resources to offer the kinds of perks to compete in Silicon Valley, but anyone can cultivate a culture that motivates and values people. All leaders can find ways to love and appreciate their people and help their people build relationships with each other. Do this and you won't just build a better work family; you'll open the door to greater success.

||

Confession time: A habit of team building is one I've struggled with my entire career. I often reasoned with myself that I was efficient and good with numbers and always on task. But looking back, I recognize that being good at other things doesn't compensate for being bad at team building. The two primary components of team building are environments and experiences, and I could have spent more time focusing on each throughout my career thus far.

I realize I can be having lots of success, growing a movement, and making a difference—yet disregarding those closest to me, which is not success. If those around me aren't flourishing, then I'm not a true leader. For those of us with a tendency to leave our feelings and emotional intelligence at home, here is a word of warning: Lack of compassion is a strong indicator of burnout about to hit. When you quit caring about your people, beware. I know this from experience.

Ask the question, "What's it like to be on the other side of me?" This leads to greater emotional intelligence, leading to improved leadership. Leadership is a choice, not a position. Be the leader you wish you had. A title or position doesn't automatically make you a leader. Influence makes you a leader. Forced followership doesn't count. People follow the person, not the position.

Leadership is not something you do to people. It's something you do for people. Care and love for your people is paramount. The best leaders are teammates, not just bosses. Leaders don't just point the way; they lead the way. Leading today requires being in the trenches with and beside your team, hands dirty helping dig the ditch. As we learned earlier, leading today means being a conductor more than a solo violinist. Active leaders alongside their team are needed, not passive leaders out in front of their team or in an ivory tower in the corner office. Your job is to shepherd, not necessarily always shine.

Poor work environments—from drama clubs to griping conventions—will sour a team as fast as anything. The problem is that leaders often blame others for a caustic workplace. They point fingers at the ringleaders and their cliques. Griping is not effective, from you or your team. But if your organization is a terrible place to work, it is your fault. The sooner you quit blaming others, the sooner you can actually fix the problems.

> 🐦 **IF YOUR ORGANIZATION IS A TERRIBLE PLACE TO WORK, IT IS YOUR FAULT. THE SOONER YOU QUIT BLAMING OTHERS, THE SOONER YOU CAN ACTUALLY FIX THE PROBLEMS.**

Find ways to create a pleasant work environment for your team. It's often the smallest touches that make the biggest differences.

- High-quality tissue paper in the bathrooms
- Free coffee
- A working copier
- Up-to-date computers
- An assortment of sweet snacks (forget the dentist; everyone loves sugar)

The second component of team building is experiences. Look for ways to create positive memories. Make sure to take a staff retreat at least once a year and take small team "field trips" no fewer than once per quarter. And whenever you engage your team like this, make it worth their time. Don't plan it last minute, and create moments of surprise along the way.

A habit of team building means a habit of creating experiences, which ultimately means a habit of fun. Find joy and happiness in the

> **IF YOU COMBINE A POSITIVE WORK ENVIRONMENT WITH REGULAR DELIGHTFUL EXPERIENCES, YOU'LL TAKE A GIANT STEP TOWARD RAISING UP A DREAM TEAM.**

everyday process. Stop and celebrate and create experiences along the way.

One of the last field trips I took my team on at Catalyst was a trip to a trampoline park. At the constant encouragement of our fun director, Chad Johnson, we looked for weeks before finding the perfect outing. Imagine a giant warehouse filled with trampolines as far as the eye can see, with a bunch of twentysomethings and thirtysomethings hopping around like kangaroos. It's basically a grown-up's dream. We jumped until we were all wet with sweat and exhausted from laughing. There's no doubt that if we had thrown something together at the last minute, the experience would have been cheapened.

If you combine a positive work environment with regular delightful experiences, you'll take a giant step toward raising up a dream team. Don't be a "have to" leader—instead be a "get to" leader. ""Get to" leaders see leading as an opportunity, not an obligation.

Many leaders *think* they are building a stronger, healthier team than they actually are. They can't see the telltale signs of dysfunction because they are too close. They don't hear the whispered conversations. They aren't privy to what their team members tell their spouses about their workdays. But that doesn't mean that a leader has no way of assessing company morale.

The best indicator of the health of a team is, and always will be, morale. If you want to measure your team's morale, take a look at turnover. Perform a 360-degree evaluation with everyone. Record the number of improvement suggestions coming from the team. Or create an anonymous poll for your team members to complete. After all, the best way to gauge someone's morale is just to ask him. You must lead people the way they want to be led, not the way you want to be led. Lead each person uniquely on your team. While you must create standards and rules, you can still customize your approach with each individual team member. Asking the opinion of your team members gives them dignity. The greatest compliment I can give to someone many times is to ask their opinion, which means asking for their input and advice.

Once you've assessed the company's morale, avoid some of these simple morale killers:

- **THE FUN POLICE**: There is at least one on every team. Their entire reason for existence is to make others feel guilty for having even a moment of fun while on the clock. Root them out and either help them grow out of it or show them the door.
- **MEETINGS GALORE**: I have never even been to your office, and I can already tell you that you have too many meetings. Sure, it makes you feel busy, but it is wasting people's time. Most people can get rid of half of their meeting calendar. If the meeting is essential, have it. If it is superfluous, scrap it. When in doubt, don't meet. Just execute. You're competent.
- **MISAPPLIED PUBLIC RECOGNITION**: When your team gets a crucial win, make sure you know who gets the credit before handing out kudos at the company picnic or staff meeting. Nothing de-motivates a team faster than misappropriated recognition.
- **UNMET PROMISES**: This is one I struggle with, and it is a surefire morale killer. Don't throw out promises you can't

keep. Period. Not even one. Hold your tongue or be prepared to deliver.

- **LACK OF SELF AWARENESS**: You must start with you: effective leaders lead themselves first. And as I learned, I'm not always that fun to be around and don't always help my team flourish. Building a team requires a courageous leader who is self-aware and self-led, and has courage to get better. You can't expect to pass on what you don't have. Your team will mirror you. If there is something you don't like, you probably created it.

> 🐦 **YOU CAN'T EXPECT TO PASS ON WHAT YOU DON'T HAVE. YOUR TEAM WILL MIRROR YOU. IF THERE IS SOMETHING YOU DON'T LIKE, YOU PROBABLY CREATED IT.**

In addition to preventing the morale killers, try a few of these morale boosters:

- **GIVE PEOPLE THE BENEFIT OF THE DOUBT**. Always believe what your people tell you unless you have reason not to. If you read that sentence and want to reply, "But she isn't trustworthy!" then you probably need to address why you have a team member you can't trust to begin with.
- **MOVE FROM "THEY" TO "WE."** Whether you're talking about another department or a team member who is not present, always opt for "we" language. If you bring on interns or volunteers, instill this in them early. The right language helps people remember that they are part of a family.
- **REMEMBER THAT WHEN THE TEAM WINS, EVERYONE WINS**. Great leaders, and great teammates, make others around them better. They are selfless and help others flourish, not just themselves. Your leadership should elevate

others and bring people together. NBA All-Star Grant Hill knows all too well that great players make their teammates better. Hill has been part of championship teams at every level. But Grant learned this at nine years old, when he scored all the points in a club basketball game. His team won 30 to 25, but Grant's dad reminded him that he may have won, but the real goal is working well with others.[3] Selfless leadership means it's not all about you.

- **BE FLEXIBLE**. I have very little to say here other than "Chill out!" Seriously. Many leaders major on the minors and minor on the majors. This kills morale. Instead, learn to be flexible in everything when it is not absolutely critical for you to be uncompromising. Candor and the ability to shoot straight should always override hierarchy on a team. Give permission to push back!

- **GIVE YOUR TEAM PERMISSION**. "You decide" is a really powerful phrase for leaders. Let people lead. Make sure your staff and everyone in your organization at all levels feel empowered and free to immediately respond to issues. Their default should be "respond and resolve," not "wait and delay." Give them the freedom to say yes. Ask your team, "What is bugging you? What are you most passionate about right now? What would you change if you were in charge?" Give them permission to not have to feel like they are whining.

- **PAY PEOPLE MORE MONEY**. I hesitate to mention this one because it is so touchy, and I'm sure that I failed here too. But ultimately, the greatest reason people will report for being unhappy is poor pay. Make sure you are at least paying your people on par with their positions according to industry standards.

Making your organization healthy is one of the top roles you have as a leader. Healthy culture provides a competitive advantage. Lots of organizations are smart but also dysfunctional, because they only focus on organizational intelligence instead of working on organizational health. Your leadership working through others is crucial. Great leaders realize that their fruit most often grows on other people's trees.

Don't assume your team knows what you need from them. If you want your team's input, be proactive and ask for it. No one assumes they should help you, so you must reach out and ask questions like "What would you like to work on?" "They" turns into "we" when people feel valued and have a voice. Getting your team bought in means your team is brought in. Circle the wagons with as many as you can, especially during times of change.

Culture building is too important to delegate. It must be taught and caught, and will end up being your fault or your fame. I recently saw this mantra on the walls at a company I was visiting, and was inspired. This is the way they see their culture:

> We lean in, get it done, have fun in the process, are the best in the world, lead out of humility, honor each other, are part of something significant and a bigger story, make each other better, have no they but we (all of us) are they, and trust one another.

In the end, you have a duty to keep people motivated and morale high. After all, you're the leader, and your words and actions weigh a thousand pounds. So if these tips don't work for you, find your own. But whatever you do, don't ignore this habit. Your organization is only as strong as its weakest team. If you build strong teams, you'll build a stronger organization. And soon you'll find that the team will almost run itself. For when you build a great team, you'll attract the kind of people who make stellar team members.

LYSA TERKEURST ON TEAM BUILDING

LYSA TERKEURST IS A BESTSELLING AUTHOR AND PRESIDENT OF PROVERBS 31 MINISTRIES.

What are you doing to inspire your team on a daily basis? Team building and leading an organization requires casting vision and constantly creating momentum. Vision must line up and connect with daily assignments. Our team has six words that define our organization and connect the vision to daily assignments: *momentum*, *word*, *wow*, *vibe*, *reality*, and *fuel*. These six words identity different departments, serve as a checklist for new opportunities, and give everyone in a department a sense of what they should own and guard.

As the team leader, it's important that I give permission to team members to dream. Our receptionist had been dreaming about an online Bible study for other women who work full time. Her goal was fifty women signing up for the online Bible study. I challenged her to double it to one hundred and agreed to let her pursue it. Well, she had twenty-two hundred women sign up!! Melissa is no longer the receptionist—she now runs the largest and fastest-growing department in Proverbs 31, with thirty-six thousand women going through her online Bible study.

If you want to be the expert on something—study it for an hour a day, a few hours per week, over five years. Then you'll become an expert. Make it something as important as a crucial appointment. If you want to be an excellent leader—you have to study other leaders and learn from them. *Momentum* became my word and area to study. What's your area to study and become an expert in? What is your word?

7 TIPS ON TEAM BUILDING FROM JOEL A'BELL

JOEL A'BELL IS THE LEAD PASTOR OF HILLSONG CHURCH IN SYDNEY, AUSTRALIA.

If a leader asked me how to develop team building in their life, I would start by making sure they understood that team building really needs to become a way of life and not just a reaction to current needs. Other than that, I would give them these seven tips:

- **ALWAYS BE LOOKING FOR PEOPLE TO HELP:** Most emerging leaders are keen to advance. They just need to be given room. Create the space for new leaders to get involved.
- **TEACH PEOPLE WHAT YOU DO:** It's always good to have more than one person who are able to do a job. The more you teach others what you do, the more you're able to give others a go.
- **MAKE ROOM FOR DIFFERENT:** Something that is different is not wrong; it's just different. I know that sounds trite, but it's true. Let people do what you have asked them to do, but let them do it the way they would like to.
- **EMPOWER THE EMPOWERMENT:** It's important to not place the expectation on your team that they actually have to do everything you want done. If they have to do everything, they will not be able to build teams themselves.
- **JUST JUMP IN AND BUILD:** Unless you're part of an environment that doesn't allow you to be more team driven, you probably don't want to work hard. Ask yourself who is missing. Key indicators would be work life balance, exhaustion, and productivity. Get the right people on the team and in the right positions.
- **LEARNING TEAM BUILDING MEANS ACTUALLY LEADING.** I like to give team members projects that are big enough to require more than just themselves to execute. My job is to simply coach them on how they are going to get this project done.

- Brian Houston often says **USE WHAT'S IN YOUR HAND TO FULFILL WHAT'S IN YOUR HEART.** It's just too easy to think about what you don't have (resource) and can't do (action) but it's a good habit to remember that God gives everything we need to do what He wants us to do.

SEVENTEEN

A HABIT OF PARTNERSHIP

COLLABORATE WITH COLLEAGUES AND COMPETITORS

In 2008, a representative from Compassion International phoned the Catalyst offices and asked to speak with me. I was familiar with their work and knew they ran a massive child sponsorship campaign, because I had seen their material at several events, including our own. I had no idea at that time how extensive their programs were—they were helping more than one million impoverished children around the world—or what they were capable of.

I would soon find out. After a brief introduction to their programs and the numerous countries where they exist, the representative paused.

"So what do you think, Brad?" he said finally. "Why don't we partner together to break the cycle of poverty?"

At first I was taken aback. I was in the event production business, not the child-saving or poverty-cycle-breaking businesses. Never before had I considered how the Catalyst brand could be leveraged for such a purpose.

Over the next several months, I began dreaming with several leaders at Compassion about collaborating for the purpose of helping children in need. The partnership seemed like a good match: they needed people to sponsor children, and we had thousands of leaders attending our events.

Over the next few years, we promoted their cause, gave them prime placement at our events, and encouraged our community to step up. One year, we brought an adult onstage who had been sponsored by Compassion. As a result of his sponsor's support, he had attended college and become a great success in life. After telling his story, we surprised him by bringing out his sponsor, whom he had never met. The man and his sponsor began to weep and collapsed on the floor. Thousands in the arena began crying with him.

That was the moment when I realized how powerful partnership can be. Thousands of children have been sponsored as a result of our collaborative relationship with Compassion. The cycle of poverty has been broken in communities around the globe because we got creative and found a way to work together. The kids who've been impacted, like the man onstage that day, aren't numbers. They are people who now don't have to worry about clean water, food, education, emotional support, and spiritual discipleship.

My point: partnerships matter.

The relationships you form with other leaders and the partnerships your organization forms with other organizations will end up producing the most significant results throughout your life.

Collaborating with others comes naturally when a leader is on his or her way up the ladder. In the early stages you *must* partner in order to progress. If you've started an organization or planted a church, you know this because you've had to outsource help. But when you reach a certain level of success, you can skirt by this. So as little fish become big ones, they need to nurture habits that force them to keep swimming in schools.

Likewise, many of the relationships and partnerships you fail to form represent the opportunities that you missed out on.

Think about the most revolutionary items you interact with in a given day. An automobile? A television set? A laptop? A smartphone? Chances are, everything at the top of your list was the product of partnerships. The idea likely arose from a brainstorming meeting. Several manufacturers partnered to make the idea into a product. And a team of distributors and salespeople worked side by side to get it into your hands.

> 🐦 **THINK ABOUT THE MOST REVOLUTIONARY ITEMS YOU INTERACT WITH IN A GIVEN DAY. CHANCES ARE, EVERYTHING AT THE TOP OF YOUR LIST WAS THE PRODUCT OF PARTNERSHIPS.**

When you work with others, your partners will recognize potential flaws you didn't see. They'll suggest improvements you wouldn't have thought of. And they'll bring skill sets and perspectives you don't have. Along the way, you'll learn new things you wouldn't otherwise have known and create a stronger idea or process or product. But most important, lives can be changed because of the partnerships you forge.

We can do more together than we can on our own. Build bridges, not walls, with others around you. There's power in partnerships. Whether a neighbor, a community initiative, a business in your community, or a conference, working together should be the norm, not the exception. Partnership should produce powerful impact.

When you have power, part of your responsibility is to share it with others. When you are the big fish in a small pond, when you're at the top, when you're the most powerful, you must be willing to stoop down and help others. You must be willing to reach across the aisle or street or barrier to collaborate. Leverage your power and influence for others' gain. Once you have a platform, you are responsible to put others on it. Remember: it's not about you.

A habit of partnership means that as a leader you are willing to come to the end of your organizational self and see a bigger vision and picture beyond just what you're working on. Be willing to sacrifice for someone else's benefit. True collaboration involves giving as much as getting.

Think of the open-source environment that has exploded online. It was all built out of a desire to collaborate and partner well. Crowdsourcing is in vogue for getting things done. Kickstarter is the essence of partnership. Amazon is allowing their customers to determine what gets green-lighted for new shows and movies. Netflix builds its online platform on an Amazon product.

A habit of partnership means learning from each other. Recently, Airbnb gathered more than fifteen hundred homeowners and hosts from forty countries for the inaugural Airbnb Open Convention in San Francisco, a free gathering for all these hosts to learn from one another and share ideas, insights, and best practices. Airbnb describes itself as a global community marketplace. Want to build a community? Make collaboration part of your DNA.

Sadly, many leaders today want to be the Lone Ranger (sans Tonto). They relish the fact that they are at the top of the organizational pyramid and prefer to make decisions without the help of others. Some of the reasons influencers resist partnerships, that I have observed, are these:

- They fear their ideas will be poached.
- They think they lack time for such endeavors.
- They don't mesh with those they'll have to work with.
- They don't want to share credit for successes.

To be fair, there *is* risk whenever you work with others. As Twyla Tharp wrote in *The Collaborative Habit*, "People are people. And people are problems. But—and this is a very big but—people who are practiced in collaboration will do better than those who insist on their individuality."[1]

The potential benefits of partnership outweigh the liabilities. The rewards exceed the risks. So go for it. But beware that partnership is hard work.

<hr />

There are many reasons a leader might form a partnership. Some are simply born out of *proximity*. The business down the street makes an item or provides a service or possesses knowledge that you need—perhaps quickly—so an alliance forms. If you had your druthers, maybe you would have worked with someone else, but this was easier, and that made it preferable.

Others arise from sheer *pragmatism*. If you own an Apple computer and run Microsoft Office for Mac, you're using a product of such a partnership. Microsoft and Apple are fierce competitors. and it is common knowledge that there is no love lost between the two entities. But Microsoft recognized that an increasing number of computer users were purchasing Macs, and Apple couldn't ignore that, despite their best efforts, customers prefer Office software. The two put their differences aside to create Microsoft software customized for Apple computers. By finding a way to work together, they've generated tens of millions in revenue and better serve both customer bases. But don't be fooled into thinking they are now more friends than foes.

Other partnerships—perhaps the best kind—are the result of a common *purpose*. Look again at the Compassion International example mentioned earlier. Catalyst seeks to holistically equip leaders, and this means providing avenues to live their faith. Compassion seeks to help children through helping Christians live their faith through generosity. An overlapping purpose led to a partnership.

The three primary impetuses for forming partnerships are listed in increasing desirability. Proximate and pragmatic partnerships *can* be healthy, but purposeful partnerships are optimal.

Regardless of how you forge alliances, it must be strategic, thoughtful, and intentional. Partnerships don't happen by osmosis. Collaboration is not coincidental. These relationships occur because someone makes a decision to form them and then invests the time and energy into managing them.

> PROXIMATE AND PRAGMATIC PARTNERSHIPS *CAN* BE HEALTHY, BUT PURPOSEFUL PARTNERSHIPS ARE OPTIMAL.

As Tharp says in *The Collaborative Habit*, "Collaborators aren't born, they're made. Or, to be more precise, built, a day at a time, through practice, through attention, through discipline, through passion and commitment—and most of all, through habit."[2]

Here are some tips for developing a habit of partnership.

- **KEEP YOUR EYES PEELED.** Some people fail to forge partnerships out of stubbornness; they miss the opportunities because they aren't paying attention. Always be on the lookout for new alliances, both inside your office and outside. When you first start developing this habit, ask yourself a question on Fridays: "Did I encounter anyone this past week who might make a valuable partner?" The more you look, the more you'll see.

- **PREFER COMPETITORS.** Most leaders can learn to work with colleagues with ease. But you should also forge partnerships with competitors. Strategic alliances with overlapping organizations—outsourcing agreements, product licensing, knowledge sharing, joint ventures— can strengthen both entities. That's why there is now a trend in competitive collaboration throughout the marketplace. Think Apple and Google. Think Amazon and Netflix. Netflix uses AWS (Amazon Web Services) and runs all of its networks and Internet connection on the framework of AWS, even though Amazon and Netflix are competitors.

a) Figure out three other leaders or organizations in your industry who are competitors whom you can serve, and work together for greater impact. Go first. Influential organizations model this.

b) Perhaps you have a product to sell. Banding together with a competitor could increase total marketplace presence and drive all sales up. At Catalyst we often advertised for other conferences at our event, and vice versa. We found that both events saw a bump in registrations.

c) Verizon, for example, is committed to what they call "co-opetition." They've formed partnerships with other content providers and software developers to create an away-from-home feature on their FiOS TV service with accompanying mobile apps. They've hosted meet-ups with developers and startups across the country to discuss challenges facing the industry.

d) Bob Mudge, president of consumer and mass business at Verizon, says of the approach, "While cooperating with other companies in your own industry may seem counterintuitive to competitiveness—the simple fact is it's not . . . Collaboration is no longer just a strategy: it is the key to long-term business success and competitiveness."[3]

- **POOL YOUR INFO.** Your goal shouldn't be just to partner with others; you should desire to encourage a collaborative culture throughout your organization. This requires pooling info and sharing contacts. I've even suggested that some organizations create a directory with contact info and expertise for potential or current partners.

- **GIVE TO GET.** No partnership—from business to marriage—is a

🐦 EXPECTATIONS ESTABLISH TRUST, SO SET THEM CLEARLY AND EARLY.

unidirectional arrangement where you reap benefits and never make sacrifices. You'll need to offer up knowledge and revenue and personnel and time in order to get back. And your partners should do likewise.

- **SET CLEAR EXPECTATIONS.** Expectations establish trust, so set them clearly and early. Define the roles and responsibilities of each party, what can and can't be shared with outsiders, and when the partnership will conclude (if ever). Make sure you *always* fulfill your end of the bargain. Trust squandered is not easily recovered, especially if you're working with an already skeptical competitor.

- **WHEN IT IS TIME TO PART, BE INTENTIONAL.** Nothing is worse than having a friend or significant other who just stops calling, texting, or e-mailing. Such behavior is hurtful and a breeding ground for bitterness. If you have the guts to begin a partnership, then have the guts to end it. And attempt to conclude the alliance in such a way that the person will speak well of you and your organization to others.

- **LET YOUNGER PEOPLE LEAD.** Today's teenagers, twentysomethings, and thirtysomethings are more willing to collaborate than any generation ever before. They trust each other, and see collaboration as the normal starting point, not some grandiose vision of teamwork that is way off in the distance. Young leaders don't care who gets the credit, and are not motivated by building their own empire, or for that matter someone else's. It's way

less about who and way more about what. Younger leaders tend to focus on "what's right" instead of "who's right"
and focus on the "best way" and not just "my way." They
see abundance, not scarcity.

A rising tide lifts all boats. When you succeed, so should others
around you. Celebrate others' success. We naturally don't cheer
others on passing us because we think it's to our demise. Lack of
unity usually comes from insecurity. It's easier to poison a well
than to dig one. Building bridges starts with actually knowing
people, even those you might compete against or disagree with.
When you are in relationship with someone, you tend to not take
shots at her. It's really hard to hate and take shots at someone up
close. When you've had a meal with someone, chances are you'll be
less likely to call him out online or in a tweet that causes him harm.
"I destroy my enemies when I make them my friends," Abraham
Lincoln once said.

Competition for customers, resources, time, and money will
always be a reality. Jealousy is natural, but how you respond to it
will prove your maturity as a leader. The best solution I've found to
combating jealousy, envy, and competition is celebration. When you
find yourself tempted to speak ill about a rival or you are secretly
wrestling with envy/jealousy over someone else you are competing with, flip that emotion on its head. Celebrate your competition.
Speak positively about them, in public and in private. Encourage
the leader or leaders of that "rival" organization. Send them cards or
notes, call them, and even visit.

Celebrating others' successes will drain the envy out of your
vessel. Unity becomes possible when we are all being tuned to the
same thing. Unity means a singular focus, from lots of different

perspectives, around one thing, like a hundred pianos tuned to the same tuning fork.

At Catalyst we could hire people internally to accomplish everything we needed, but instead, we sought external help for many of our critical components. For example, Catalyst is known for high-quality creations—logos, original videos, event production, and so forth. Most of Catalyst's creative ingenuity was greatly enhanced by key people *outside* of Catalyst. We sought out the most creative people in the world, realizing they wouldn't join us full-time, but might be willing to partner. This gave us opportunity to work with people who have done great work in many fields, therefore bringing a large skill set and exposure to bear on projects.

Unfortunately, one sector that doesn't do this well but should is the church. The church should be the most collaborative institution and industry in the world, because the basis of the church is love. Love is generous and selfless. But often, we have a scarcity mentality and tend to hoard and protect. The bottom line: getting things done today and in the future will require working together. "You can do what I cannot do. I can do what you cannot do," said Mother Teresa. "Together we can do great things."

In 1986, Michael Jordan began winning scoring titles in the National Basketball Association. But Jordan's team, the Chicago Bulls, wasn't winning championships. Phil Jackson, the Chicago Bulls' head coach, explained why: "Scoring champions don't win championships."

In other words, success requires the effort of many working together.

Jackson began working to recruit players at key positions who could work alongside Jordan. And he began making Jordan move the ball around to his teammates. In 1991, the Chicago Bulls won their first championship with Jordan and the first in franchise history. Jordan was voted MVP in the finals that year, a game in which he scored 30 points and racked up ten assists.[4]

As in basketball, so in business. Success is produced by teams of people working together, not Lone Ranger leaders riding off into the sunset. You must learn to collaborate with colleagues and competitors if you want to be a change maker.

I know that might sound daunting—it may be the scariest of all the habits—but to put it bluntly: You don't have a choice. In today's interconnected, global economy, collaboration is the norm. Those who *don't* or *won't* form partnerships will sink; those who *do* will soar.

JEFF SLOBOTSKI ON PARTNERSHIP

JEFF SLOBOTSKI IS FOUNDER OF BIG OMAHA, BIG KANSAS CITY, SILICON PRAIRIE NEWS, AND ROUTER VENTURES.

To develop a habit of collaboration and partnership, I constantly reconnect with people in my network that I may not have visited with for some time. There's no "ask" when I touch base. It's just a check-in to see how things are going and if there's anything I can do for them or people I can connect them with.

Helping others is critical. Leaders should look [for] which resources they can offer to help others. They should take time to look introspectively, identify what they are good at, and then share it with others. This requires developing a "giving mind-set" instead of a "taking mind-set" where you're trying to determine what you can get from someone else.

6 TIPS ON COLLABORATION FROM BOBBY GRUENEWALD

BOBBY GRUENEWALD IS INNOVATION LEADER AT LIFECHURCH.TV AND COFOUNDER OF THE YOUVERSION BIBLE APP.

I think one of the most important factors for collaborative success is to understand what collaboration isn't. Collaboration isn't groupthink. It isn't trying to get everybody's opinion or buy-in at every step of the way. At its best, collaboration means bringing together people and teams with diverse gifts and allowing them to contribute from their strengths.

It is be difficult to recommend a one-size-fits-all approach to collaboration since everyone is going to have a unique set of circumstances. But here are some general tips and advice to help people develop a habit of collaboration:

- **GET CLARITY ON THE PROBLEM TO BE SOLVED.** Collaboration for the sake of collaboration is problematic if there's not clarity around what you're trying to accomplish together.
- **GET INPUT ON A PROJECT FROM A VARIETY OF PEOPLE**—even those you don't get along with well.
- **DISCUSS COLLABORATION WITH YOUR TEAM.** I meet with my teams regularly, and one of our recurring agenda items is to talk about how they are working with other teams. We get to celebrate collaborations that are working well, and we also talk about how we can get back on track when it isn't flowing.
- **WHEN SEVERAL TEAMS ARE WORKING ON A PROJECT, I'M A BIG FAN OF CLARIFYING QUESTIONS:** *Who's going to own that? When did they say they are going to have that done? Are you sure they know that?* I've seen too many projects fall apart when team members aren't clear on who's doing what by when.
- **WORK TO WEAVE COLLABORATION INTO YOUR ENTIRE CULTURE.** At LifeChurch.tv, God has created each church with a unique blend of people and resources, so when we start to tackle a big goal, our instinct is to look for partners who can contribute from their gifts and strengths.
- **CREATE AN ENVIRONMENT OF TEAM ACCOUNTABILITY FOR COLLABORATION.** Make it a checkpoint in project discussions: did you give other team members an opportunity to weigh in on a decision that affects them? If not, pause the discussion until you can loop in the appropriate people.

JOSHUA DUBOIS ON PARTNERSHIP

JOSHUA DUBOIS IS THE AUTHOR OF *THE PRESIDENT'S DEVOTIONAL* AND FORMER DIRECTOR OF FAITH-BASED PARTNERSHIPS FOR THE WHITE HOUSE.

Forging partnerships is tough, but I try to make time for open-ended relationships that lead to them: coffees, lunches, dinners where there is no specific objective other than to hear from the other person. Partnership can very easily feel and seem transactional, so whenever possible I start by building a relationship first. I try to listen before I pitch a partnership. *What do they need? What are the holes they're seeking to fill?* I try not to assume that my goal is their goal.

Once a partnership forms, I let the content of meetings drive the length instead of the other way around. This helps create spaces for genuine collaboration. If we're done in three minutes, great. If, in order to make sure everyone is heard and all opportunities are on the table, we have to go 90 minutes, that's fine too.

If someone wants to develop a habit of partnership, they might start by meeting with a leader from a completely different sector and background every week. If a leader works in the church, for example, they might meet with someone from the business sector. If in business, they could meet with someone in politics. If in politics, they could meet with someone in nonprofit work. Also, I suggest varying these meetings by race, ethnicity, and other lines of division. An impulse toward broadened horizons is invaluable when developing a habit of partnership.

EIGHTEEN

A HABIT OF MARGIN

NURTURE HEALTHIER RHYTHMS

Watching my sabbatical's end approach was like witnessing a sunrise. The anticipation of the glowing orb of a new day flooded my veins with adrenaline, while saying good-bye to the peacefulness of my starlit season was difficult.

I had decided to continue consulting and serving as a strategic advisor with Catalyst, but I would now be mostly self-employed. Though I was something of my own boss before my sabbatical, the daily accountability of a physical team would no longer be there. But I didn't want to go back to the way it was—there's a reason I needed the sabbatical in the first place; instead I wanted to take all I had learned in the last decade and create a healthier life.

Before taking my sabbatical, my life's rhythms sounded like a twelve-year-old practicing his scales on a saxophone. On occasion the sound was pleasant, but the off-pitch bleats at the most unpredictable times threw the whole package off.

Sure, I had experienced much success in my career. But I had stopped allotting time for the activities I enjoyed—hunting, skiing, golfing, fishing, reading, and more—so my life wasn't much fun.

Weekends had become a time to get more work done so I could get ahead of everyone else. My lifelong friendships had grown strained and were getting little attention. I wasn't exercising, and my diet consisted of as many desserts as fresh vegetables. Everything was "urgent." I wasn't sleeping well, and as a result, was often cranky. Post-sabbatical Brad wouldn't even want to hang out with pre-sabbatical Brad. A new person had truly emerged out of this time. But in many ways it was returning to a Brad that had been lost and needed to be found once again.

Stopping to slow down allowed me to get my smile back. Many of us take pride in being stressed, overworked, anxious, and burned-out. Our answer is constantly "I'm really busy." What if our answer was "I'm rested and rejuvenated." Sabbaticals, rest, margin, and rhythm seem like falling behind, or losing the edge of your game. Even peers within your organization might think you're lazy or just looking for an excuse to take more time away. But not being willing to stop, reflect, and recharge because you feel you've got to get ahead and you can't lose ground is a losing proposition.

> 🐦 **THE MORE MARGIN IN YOUR LIFE, THE MORE ROOM YOU HAVE TO LET YOUR RHYTHMS RUN.**

The goal of my reordering was not just to create a better schedule, but to create margin. The more margin in your life, the more room you have to let your rhythms run.

Margin is a powerful habit. It creates opportunities. For businesses, margin creates profit. Margin in family creates memories and in personal finances creates generosity. Margin in our friendships creates significance and in our lives overall creates options—options to pursue dreams, think, pray, process, grow, and ultimately live and lead more fully. For all of us, time is our greatest asset. We can't create more of it. We have to make sure we are using it wisely, and margin allows us to leverage time effectively.

There are three components of margin:

1. *Stillness*: If you're a type-A leader or have a touch of adult ADD or pretty much are like anyone I know, just sitting still can be difficult. In fact, according to *Entrepreneur* magazine, more people would rather get shocked than sit in stillness for fifteen minutes.

   Listen carefully: Don't. Give. Up. Learning to unwind is a discipline that must be practiced. You must find time to stop moving, stop working, and stop problem solving.

   Even Jesus practiced stillness. The Gospels often talk about Jesus rising in the morning to retreat to a quiet place. Away from the crowds, away from the disciples, just to be still and alone with God. In fact, it was because of this stillness that He was able to do such effective work and ministry. He was the living embodiment of Psalm 1:3: "He will be like a tree firmly planted by streams of water, which yields its fruit in its season" (NASB). Leaders should strive to imitate His example. We all need solitude. Quiet allows for you to hear God.

2. *Sabbath*: Many people think of Sabbath as nothing more than rest time, but this is not completely correct. Sabbath means pausing *so that* you can connect with God. As theologian Walter Brueggemann has said, "Sabbath means to be in a mode of receptivity for gifts to be given and that requires one to slow down, to pause, to wait."[1] Set a regular time each week for this, and fight to protect it.

3. *Space*: A common synonym for *margin* is actually *space*. This means that once everything is scheduled, this is what is left over. Many leaders have no space. Every moment of their weeks is scheduled—probably overbooked. Invest

the energy to carve out unscheduled time within your schedule.

My sabbatical served as a hard reset, like simultaneously hitting the power and home page buttons on your phone. With so much of the noise and obligation gone, I could see clearly again. I knew more about how "music" of life should sound now and wanted to reengineer my daily rhythms.

If you don't control your cadence, your cadence will control you.

We have to limit the distractions. If you're like me, when I have my computer on, I usually have fifteen to twenty different windows open. But when needing to focus, I have to close these windows or otherwise I get distracted. Same with life. We need to close some of the "open windows" in our lives, which will allow our brains and souls to

> **🐦 IF YOU DON'T CONTROL YOUR CADENCE, YOUR CADENCE WILL CONTROL YOU.**

run faster. Limit the distractions so we can focus in on what is in front of us. At some point too many windows open just shuts down our computers, and ourselves.

The tempo of many leaders' lives sounds like mine used to. It is chaotic and random, pitchy and painful. These influencers will often report that they feel stressed by their schedules, but they can't tell you their strategy for getting them under control. How does one develop healthier rhythms?

For an analogy of how to do this, I always think back to my days at Lost Valley Ranch. If you have a wild horse that is running and bucking and giving you fits, and you need to get it under control, you'll need to lasso it in. A wild life-rhythm is like a wild stallion. Reining it in will require learning to use a rope called "time management."

This term often induces groans and eye rolls, but it is necessary and unavoidable if you want to develop a habit of margin. If you have let your life's rhythms get out of control, here are a few tips for better managing your time.

- **START BY RECORDING.** You won't know how to manage your time if you don't know what you spend your time doing. For the first week or two, carry a schedule and write down everything you spend time doing. Be prepared to be surprised. You'll never guess what captivates your time.
- **SKETCH A SCHEDULE.** Once you know how much time you spend on each task, set aside a maximum limit for each action. The interesting thing about time management is that you'll often complete any task in the time you allot for it. If you give yourself three hours to write a speech, you'll spend three hours. If you give yourself one hour, that's what you'll invest. And even more interestingly, you may find the quality isn't noticeably different.
- **PRIORITIZE FOR PRODUCTIVITY.** Look at your schedule of regular activities and then ask, "Am I devoting the most time and energy to the most important items on the list?" If not, make adjustments. And those items that you know deep down shouldn't be on the list . . . quit doing them!
- **INCLUDE INTERRUPTIONS.** If you think something will take you an hour, it won't. At least not every time, because life is full of interruptions. Get your activities down as lean as you think you can take them, and then add 5 percent for interruptions.
- **HAVE FUN AND ENJOY THE PROCESS.** Part of making sure your smile stays in place is making time to do the things

you love. For me, it's duck hunting, golf, and snow skiing. Lean into the things that you love to do, things that re-energize you and bring you to life.

- **REMEMBER TO REST.** Sabbath and stillness are core components of margin; they must be hammered into your schedule. They will not happen naturally, and your tendency will be to strike them first when life gets busy. Rest needs to be a high-priority item in your calendar. I suggest 20 percent of all scheduled time being devoted to activities that help you unwind. If you're hustling but not resting, you need to rework your schedule.

- **COMMIT TO THE "THREE F'S."** In addition to rest, you need to make sure that you devote ample time to your *friends* and *family* and *faith*. You can lose your job tomorrow, but the three F's will remain. So build barriers to protect them. Make life's permanent things a permanent priority.

> 🐦 **MAKE LIFE'S PERMANENT THINGS A PERMANENT PRIORITY.**

- **MAKE SLEEP A PRIORITY.** Many want to brag about their ability to go for long periods of time without enough sleep. But it's not healthy. Our bodies need to slow down. Even race-car drivers understand the importance of slowing down. You have to slow down to go around the corner in order to speed up through the straight stretches.

- **REMEMBER: FRESH VISION IS A RESULT OF A FRESH MIND.** You want fresh vision for your organization, your church, your business, or your ministry? Find margin. Many times fresh vision is fueled from a time of rest and recharging. Vision requires stepping back and gaining perspective, not grinding through with a mind that is scattered, distracted, and stressed.

- **DON'T EAT YOUR EXTRA.** Remember that the goal of time
management is a habit of *margin*. Once you've gotten your
schedule down to the leanest form possible, the leftover
is margin. Mentally stick a sign on it that reads, "Not for
sale." That leftover allows for being present during interruptions and moments of inconvenience, which can be
moments when God does the greatest work through us.

As I reentered the workplace, I was already beginning to nurture
healthier rhythms. My schedule was honed, and I was highly productive. Yet I also found time for stillness, Sabbath, and space.

With my newfound margin, I found time to have spontaneous
lunches with friends, fly-fish, hunt, travel, play golf, stay an extra
day, extend the conversation, and connect on a deeper level. I would
never have done these things before. I would have replied to any
invitations with, "I'm sorry. I just can't take the time." And if someone managed to convince me to go, I would have been overrun with
guilt. Now I knew that such activities weren't *indulgent*; they were
investing in a healthier tempo. I've also built in a habit of forty-five
minutes per day for exercise, which has resulted in me losing thirty-
five pounds. And it also allows more time to think, pray, listen to
podcasts, and dream.

A couple of months after my sabbatical ended, television producer Mark Burnett invited me to fly to Los Angeles and be a guest
for the finals of *The Voice*. I agreed to come and called my seventeen-
year-old niece, Carlee. She loves Adam Levine. When I told her I
wanted to take her with me, she reacted much as you'd expect: she
freaked out.

Carlee is from Bristow, Oklahoma, a small farm town, and had
never visited the West Coast before. I flew her out early to get the full

LA experience. We visited the Griffith Observatory and the Santa Monica Pier. I even took her to the Giving Keys office because she loves Caitlin Crosby.

On the day of *The Voice* finals, we were driven to the studio in a golf cart and ushered into the green room. We were given VIP tickets and were allowed to sit in the famous red chairs before the show started. When the show commenced and the stage lights turned on, I looked over at Carlee's wide eyes and knew we were making a memory that would last a lifetime.

Before my sabbatical, I might have flown out for a day but wouldn't have spent nearly a week in Los Angeles. I would've worked most of the time I was there. But now I had margin, and that changed everything. Margin creates moments; it makes life more meaningful. Margin creates space for magic to happen.

One day, Carlee will tell her children about how Uncle Brad took her to the West Coast for the first time. She'll remember the places we visited and the food we ate and the fun we had. My memory will live on in the tales she'll tell. And it would never have happened without a habit of margin.

Make time for margin.

CRAIG GROESCHEL ON MARGIN

CRAIG GROESCHEL IS PASTOR OF LIFECHURCH.TV AND A BEST-SELLING AUTHOR.

Some people define rest as "not doing work." But I think of rest in broader terms. Rest, to me, can mean "not working"; but it also means doing something that brings replenishment to my body, mind, or soul. For example, when I work out, my mind is resting. So I have a commitment to leave the office daily at 3:45 to work out at 4:00. Not only does it give my mind a break, it helps me to sleep better at night. Exercise is a form of rest.

You have to guard the time that you rest and replenish. Guarding my day off is a gigantic priority. In the past, my day off often got absorbed by some emergency or opportunity probably half the time or more. As I've grown in my leadership, I've learned that I could delegate most of the emergencies to someone else, and saying no to many "opportunities" is more important than losing a true day of rest.

For deeper rest personally, I take longer breaks. To me, two consecutive weeks off isn't twice as good as one, it's way more than that. Since it often takes several days to decompress, the best rest is almost always in a second week away from work.

As for margin with the family, we block out Tuesday night as family night. With six kids, if we are not careful, we will not have any evenings with everyone here. Even my older two girls (who have moved out) block this night off and come home for dinner and family time.

Guard your margin.

NINETEEN

A HABIT OF GENEROSITY

LEAVE THE WORLD A BETTER PLACE

The sinking feeling in my gut felt like a mixture of stomach flu and hunger pains. The possibility of personnel changes is always difficult, but this one was especially hard given that the "personnel" was a highly gifted and competent close friend of mine.

I met Reggie Joiner more than a decade ago. Good ideas oozed from his mind onto everyone he encountered. For years Reggie emceed Catalyst's concept and creative meetings. He would enter a meeting with a black pin board and neon colored index cards. Before we finished, the board was filled with names and ideas flashing like strobe lights. Reggie Joiner was invaluable to our organization, and I have no qualms about saying that Catalyst would not be what it is today without him.

One day, however, I began realizing that the organization needed a makeover, not because we weren't successful or failing to execute, but because every organization needs to be shaken up on occasion in order to stay fresh. The idea that we needed to configure our key leaders and bring in fresh thinkers started keeping me awake at night.

As I discussed my thinking with Reggie, it became clear to both of us that we might benefit from a transition in some of the roles he had been filling. And that's when the most amazing thing happened. Reggie *came to me*.

"I have loved being a part of this team, and it has been a great honor," he said. "But I know it is time for a transition and to give someone else a chance to try their hand. I'm going to make this decision easy for you and step aside."

In that moment I knew that Reggie Joiner was more than talented and creative. He was one of the most self-aware, mature, and brave leaders I've met. He knew that making room for fresh leaders is not a statement on one's competency but a necessary part of keeping an organization's edges sharp. The day I made the same decision and gave up my chair at Catalyst, I thought about Reggie and his example. The graciousness he displayed when making his decision gave me strength to face my own.

Reggie's response was born out of a spirit of generosity, something that permeates his entire life. If you mention you like his shoes, he's the kind of guy who very well may have a pair for you next time you see him. I've never had a meal with him that he didn't pay for. He'll meet with almost anybody if his schedule allows. Once, a member of the Catalyst creative team needed a computer, and Reggie bought it for him.

When a transition was needed, Reggie knew that he didn't own anything and that God had loaned him everything. Because he saw his role as an opportunity to be stewarded, he was happy to give it away to another leader. Even after Reggie transitioned off the team, he and his organization, Orange, continued to promote Catalyst. Talk about classy!

In a capitalistic culture the word *generosity* has a fiscal connotation. And that is fitting. But generosity is more than how one stewards and spends money; it's a holistic posture that should animate everything a leader does. The more you have, the harder it is to pass it on.

As Erika Andersen, *Forbes* columnist, says, "Leaders quite often confuse being generous with giving people money—raises, bonuses, stock options. . . . [But] the generous leader gives people what they truly want: knowledge, power, information, credit, praise, responsibility and authority."[1]

Actually, if you read Daniel Pink's widely regarded book, *Drive: The Surprising Truth About What Motivates Us* (Riverhead Books, 2011), you know that research indicates money isn't the motivator we often assume. It's not as simple as "pay people more money and everybody is happier." People want more from their leaders than a fatter paycheck.

Whatever you possess—the classic formulation is "time, treasure, talent"—should be given away liberally and not hoarded. *This* is what a habit of generosity looks like, and it is one of the best ways to ensure you'll leave the world a better place than you found it.

In business, relationships, networks, platforms, technology, distribution, conferences, content delivery, and strategic partnership, the rising standard is open source. This new wave of leaders have tools such as Twitter, Facebook, LinkedIn, YouTube, Instagram, Snapchat, and many more social media outlets that make influence through sharing readily available. Social media is actually built on a premise that the more you share and are generous, the more influence you'll gain.

> 🐦 GENEROSITY IS MORE THAN HOW ONE SPENDS MONEY; IT'S A HOLISTIC POSTURE THAT SHOULD ANIMATE EVERYTHING A LEADER DOES.

Want to gain more Twitter followers? Share and be generous with others' content. Want more Facebook likes? Talk about someone else and share more great content links with your fans. Share ideas, links, friends, and networks. This is a complete paradigm shift in the last twenty years because of technology and online networks.

A habit of generosity also means we are invested. It doesn't mean we just "like" a new justice cause on Facebook, or put on a wristband, or only pour ice water over our heads and post it on Twitter. We can easily "like" something but not be invested in it. This is a big issue with my generation and the generation coming up behind me. Are we changing the world, or just trying to make ourselves feel good? We have to fight against the idea of just wearing a wristband and feeling as if we've done something.

The good news is that generosity is in vogue. Generosity is a habit that others want to emulate and that culture appreciates. Generosity and sharing are the new currencies of our culture. True success means helping others be successful, and getting ahead means helping others get ahead. Creating wins for others is more fun, and ultimately very strategic.

For me it always begins and ends around the issue of stewardship, which describes the act of watching over someone else's things. It helps remind me that I am not the owner, but only the manager of all I have. In this way of thinking, we take what we have been given and look after it with intentionality. Be faithful with where you are and what you've been given.

The foundation of generosity is people. Whether you are sharing information or love or wealth, there is a person who is offering it and a person who is receiving it. In his groundbreaking book, *Give and Take*, business professor Adam Grant explored the topic of generosity.

Even before conducting his research, he knew that successful people held three things in common: motivation, ability, and opportunity. But his research showed that there's a "critical yet often neglected . . . fourth ingredient" that profoundly influences high achievement: "how we approach interactions with other people."[2]

Most leaders fall into one of three categories: *Takers* get more than they give. *Matchers* give to others expecting something in return. *Givers* offer to others without considering payback. I'll go out on a limb here and say that most of your team wants to work for and with a serial giver rather than a serial taker. So which are you?

- **LISTEN TO YOUR LANGUAGE:** Do you speak more of "me" or "we"?
- **CONSIDER YOUR TACTICS:** Do you operate on fear and suspicion or trust?
- **LOOK AT YOUR BUDGET:** Do you invest more in institutional growth or improving the lives of your people and clients?
- **INSPECT YOUR DAILY SCHEDULE:** Do you spend more time giving to others or asking from others?
- **OBSERVE YOUR CULTURE:** Are your relationships strong or strained? Are you creating community or controlling a corporation?

> 🐦 **MOST OF YOUR TEAM WANTS TO WORK FOR AND WITH A SERIAL GIVER RATHER THAN A SERIAL TAKER.**

These types of questions will help you begin to diagnose whether your leadership is marked by generosity or selfishness.

Most of us—even if we aren't full-on takers or selfish in every aspect—have elements of our leadership that could be more generous. For example, I'm frugal and have a difficult time giving money to people if I think I can steward it better than they. Depending on the circumstance, I'd rather take someone to lunch and give him advice than give him money without knowing how it would be spent. I forget that when we are financially generous, it is as much to grow us into giving people as it is to help someone who needs resources.

But some of my closest friends are the opposite. They don't want to be bothered with you, thank you very much. They are busy people. If a donation will make you go away or make them feel better about themselves, they'll happily pay it. Both they and I need to be aware of how we are selfish, even if we're generous in other ways. We all need to set goals to challenge us in this way.

A habit of generosity requires head, heart, hands, and feet. Generosity means service and focusing on others. Generosity turns *me* into *we*. As Andy Stanley says, "the value of a life is always measured by how much of it was given away. At funerals we never celebrate accumulation. We may envy accumulation, but we always celebrate generosity and selflessness. At the end of your life that is what is celebrated. Life's got to be beyond you, not about you."[3]

A few years ago, I woke up to the need to be more financially generous. I decided to commit to giving a million dollars to charity over the course of my life. Now, for those of you who think I make more money than I actually do, let me assure you: this has meant a lot of sacrifice to even begin chipping away at it.

This focus on financial generosity really started when a good friend of mine, Daryl Heald, challenged me fifteen years ago. We were in a concept meeting for a magazine called *Life@Work* and doing a magazine issue on the topic of giving. Daryl challenged me and our team on the idea that financial generosity demonstrates a level of maturity in someone's faith life. I was convicted. At twenty-six, I hadn't been giving much at all up to that point in my life. Just basically "tipping" God. I had to make some sacrifices and start making this a priority.

I want to be remembered as someone who passed on what I had to others, who never said no when God had a "yes" for me, and who was faithful and generous with what he was given. And this means being intentionally generous in a way that stretches and stings a little. You can give without loving, but you can't love without giving. You haven't learned how to truly live until you learn how to truly give.

How does one develop a habit of generosity, practically speaking? Here are a few tips.

- **BE GENEROUS WITH POWER.** What do you do with the authority and responsibility you have been given? Some people hoard it and become organizational pack rats. But generous leaders learn to offer it to others. Would a younger, more inexperienced leader benefit from taking the reins on a project for a while? Give it away. Would someone else learn a few leadership lessons from having a higher level of authority? Delegate to her. If you are a leader who is generous with power, those above you will trust you with more of it. Use your platform to help others and put others on it. Loan your power and influence liberally. The more influence and power you have, the more responsibility you have to use it for the betterment of others.

- **BE GENEROUS WITH TIME.** I know leaders who rush in and out of meetings, and their team members have to muster the courage to even tug on their sleeves. Make sure you give liberally of your time. If someone is struggling or has a death in the family, don't just send a fruit basket. Sit and listen to his pain for a moment. If the entire team is pulling an all-nighter, don't go home to your family while they have to remain. Choose to stay late and pitch in. Time is one of the top commodities that generous leaders must learn to gift.

- **BE GENEROUS WITH EXPERTISE.** Every leader has a certain skill set and knowledge base, which is what I'm calling expertise. It's the talent factor. This is acquired through education (particularly for younger leaders), experience (particularly for older leaders), and ongoing learning (particularly for bookworms and conference junkies). Regardless, all the expertise is sloshing around in a leader's head, but the most generous ones will pour it out onto those around them.

  This type of generosity requires a confident leader who is comfortable in his or her skin, because giving away expertise may make you feel less valuable. "If everyone knows what I know," you might say to yourself, "then I'll be expendable to them." Actually, the opposite is true. Everyone wants to keep those who are generous with expertise around because they are a gift to all. Once you become the expert, your responsibility is to give away what you know.

- **BE GENEROUS WITH PRAISE.** People may forget whether you had pretzel sticks at the Christmas party, but they will remember if you praise them. I must admit, I was a poor praiser for many years, and I still struggle to offer encouragement. It makes me feel awkward and vulnerable. But I've never given up trying, because I know it matters and is a critical component of generous leadership.

- **BE GENEROUS WITH ACCESS:** Can your people get to you when they need you? I know of several leaders who have special e-mail addresses and blocked cell phone numbers that their team members don't know. These leaders may have reserved parking spots and private entrances. When they are in the office, their team doesn't feel the freedom to enter if they would like to talk. This is selfish leadership.

Don't have a middleman (or "middlewoman," as it were) whom everyone must go through to access you. Remind your people that you are available, even if you have to maintain due process or chain of command when resolving issues. Maintain an open-door policy, at least during part of the week. You have no chance of being a generous leader if you're an insulated leader.

> **YOU HAVE NO CHANCE OF BEING A GENEROUS LEADER IF YOU'RE AN INSULATED LEADER.**

If you make these practices second nature, you'll be shocked at how much they will pay off. Generous leaders attract and retain top-notch talent. They attract high-quality, loyal partners. They end up with reputations that others revere. And they construct a lasting legacy. Serving, sweating, and sacrificing leads to influence, significance, and ultimate success.

As Adam Grant concluded in *Give and Take*, what Christians believe about life turns out to be true for leaders: "For it is in giving that we receive."

FIVE TIPS ON GENEROSITY BY TODD AND SUSAN PETERSON

TODD PETERSON PLAYED IN THE NFL FOR MORE THAN TEN YEARS, AND SUSAN PETERSON SERVES ON THE NATIONAL BOARD OF YOUNG LIFE.

- Humble yourself before God daily and understand all you have and are is a result of His generosity in the first place. Ask the Holy Spirit to do in you what you can't do alone: make you generous.
- Say "no" to yourself (your desires and wants) so you can say "yes" to others' needs.
- Try to serve someone six times before asking them for something.
- Always give a little more than you planned to give.
- Pick a lifestyle early on and stick with it throughout life. As your income increases over time, don't let your lifestyle creep up just because you have more capacity.

TWENTY

A HABIT OF SUCCESSION

FIND POWER IN PASSING THE BATON

"You got your smile back."

This is what my friends and team told me after my sabbatical concluded, and I knew they were right. One year earlier, I sat in the same room at the Catalyst office, out of gas and coasting on fumes. My leadership was stale and my heart was strained. My smile was gone.

But now my mind is cloudless; my energy is high; my muscles are more relaxed. I feel alive again. To borrow a phrase from Johnny Nash, I can see clearly now the rain is gone. Now I just need to learn how to live with the new life I was creating. A life where I wasn't the one calling the shots anymore. A life without being in charge.

I'm proud of the work I accomplished those many years I served the Catalyst community. I saw hundreds of thousands of leaders inspired and encouraged. I watched many refuel and recommit to going back into their spheres of influence to make the world a better place. Along the way, I learned a lot about how to lead, how not to lead, who I am, and who I am not. I defined my leadership DNA, and then I passed the essence of that DNA into my team, so that when the time was right, I could release it to them.

Too many leaders grab their jobs with an unrelenting death grip. But part of every influencer's responsibility is to boldly build something magnificent and then humbly hand it off to others. The best leaders recognize this early on, creating a pipeline of leadership that transfers responsibilities and power to the next wave, the next line, the next team, so that others can take what you've accomplished and build on it in their own way.

> **THE BEST WAY TO SHORE UP YOUR LEGACY IS TO EFFECTIVELY HAND IT OFF TO YOUR SUCCESSORS.**

Surprisingly, the best way to shore up your legacy is to effectively hand it off to your successors. Part of our responsibility is to pass the torch—success requires succession. Great leaders ultimately get out of the way. There is power in passing on.

Frank Blake was CEO of Home Depot for seven years, a time during which the company grew and flourished and racked up a host of wins. Under his watch, Home Depot experienced a 127 percent increase in share price. But on his first day in the position, January 3, 2007, he was already thinking about the day he would depart. At his very first board meeting, he began conversations about succession planning and how to promote from within to cultivate a strong team of leaders below him.

Under Blake's leadership, the board devoted two annual meetings to talent reviews and succession planning. This made life easy when, in 2013, he began talking about retirement. The board identified three contenders to succeed Blake, and they committed to maintaining the dignity of each throughout the process. When it was time to go, he handed off his role to Craig Menear with hardly a hitch. The company's stock price didn't even vibrate. He left admired and on top.

"[Blake] is one of the finest human beings I have ever been blessed to know," Ken Langone, one of the company's founders, would say of him.[1]

One of the most difficult lessons for leaders to learn is how to let go. Often, we leave kicking and screaming, if not on the outside, then in our hearts and minds. We cheer our team as we depart, but we secretly hope they crash and burn. *Then everyone will know how critical I was to their success.*

Every influencer struggles with leadership transfer, and no one should be ashamed about admitting it. If it hurts to let something go, it just means that you've come to love it. And the longer you've loved, the harder it is to say good-bye.

🐦 **ONE OF THE MOST DIFFICULT LESSONS FOR LEADERS TO LEARN IS HOW TO LET GO.**

It would be a lie to say that I didn't wrestle with this decision. The thought of charting a path into an unknown future unsettled me. I'm not the first leader to struggle with succession. Given enough time, most every influencer reaches a place where he or she is too deep, too invested, and too tired to continue at the current pace. Sadly, many are too stubborn or too egotistical or too afraid to do what they know is needed when they arrive at this waypoint. They need to step out so that others can step up. But they don't.

A close friend of mine made a similar mistake a couple of years ago, choosing to press on rather than pass the baton. His organization languished as a result. Just shy of utter ruin, he was forced out, and his staff was left behind to sort through the wreckage. I determined at that moment never to allow myself to reach the same point. I decided I was going to step aside before I needed to and move on before I was asked.

I had been thinking about my departure from Catalyst off and on for years. I didn't know the day I would need to step aside, but I knew it was approaching. I began to promote from within, to hand off responsibility, and even to consider hiring someone to work alongside me for a time.

But I now realize I should have been *more* intentional. Even though I had a fairly seamless succession, it could have been smoother. With more planning, more input, and more intentionality, my departure could have looked more like Frank Blake's. That's why when I coach prominent leaders today, I usually talk through their succession plans. (Most don't have one at all.)

The process of succession begins with asking difficult questions. And these queries should be considered with the help of a team of trusted advisors. *Is it time for me to move on? Who is being groomed to replace me and those under me? Who can help us identify the right people for the right roles with fresh perspective?*

As you ask these questions, consider the following tips in helping you develop a habit of succession. I wish someone had shared these with me early in my career.

- **START SOONER THAN YOU THINK YOU SHOULD.** The time to find a successor is never when you need one. Not to be grim, but your organization is one fatal car accident from disaster. Plan before you need to so that whenever the day arrives, you'll be ready. Pass the baton before *you* think it needs to be passed.
- **ASSEMBLE A TRUSTED TASK FORCE.** You need help planning for succession, but it must be the right kind of help. Transition planning can make you vulnerable as a leader, so make sure you surround yourself with *trusted* advisors who can speak honestly with you but won't stab you in the back when you aren't looking.
- **LET GO SLOWLY BUT STEADILY.** As you begin to see the day of departure coming, peel back slowly from your roles

and responsibility. Take your replacement leaders to board meetings, on trips, and to site visits. Don't let go of the steering wheel in a single, unbridled moment. This will help the person who will take over your position ease into the role and the rest of the team grow comfortable with his or her style.

- **GET REAL-TIME FEEDBACK, AND ADJUST AS NECESSARY.** No leader gets it right at the start every time. Allow your task force to evaluate the transition in real time. When adjustments—even significant ones that set you back—are necessary, make them.

- **REMEMBER THAT YOU NEED TO BE REPLACED BY A WHOLE TEAM, WORKING TOGETHER, NOT A SINGLE PERSON.** Consider new roles that may need to be created or old roles that need to be eliminated or reassigned according to the forthcoming structure. Succession is not a brain transplant, but a body transformation. Evaluate from feet to haircut.

- **SET A STRICT DEADLINE.** Without a deadline, your plan runs the risk of dragging on forever. So set a firm deadline and plan to end ahead of schedule—that way any setbacks or adjustments won't derail the whole process. This deadline is nonnegotiable and unmovable. If you aren't ready when it arrives, let go anyway. Your assessment that the team isn't ready might just be your reticence to leave. Execute the plan.

- **GET OUT OF THE WAY.** When it is time to go, leave. Some leaders can remain a part of the organization in a carefully defined role, but you cannot play a key part in day-to-day operations. It's confusing for the team and you may be tempted to sabotage operations. Leave and leave with dignity, and speak well and honor the new leader and team once you've stepped aside.

- **BEGIN AGAIN.** Transition doesn't mean you are through. Reimagine new leadership, a new role, and a new life. You don't need to run away; you just need to get out of the way.

The legacy of your influence relies significantly, though not completely, on how well the organization thrives *after* you leave. Consider your replacements a direct reflection on the quality of your leadership. Raising up young leaders is a waste of time unless you put them into roles where they can lead and ultimately take over.

The ceiling of one generation is the floor to the next. Stand on what's already been built by those before you. Then see your role as building a foundation for those who show up behind you in the next generation to carry what you've already helped build.

I'm writing this one year removed from my role as president of Catalyst. I remain in a limited advisory role, but one with healthy distance and clear boundaries. The baton has been passed to a team of highly capable leaders who are building their own organization and breathing new life into a vital movement.

Today, things are different even though they are the same.

When I attend Catalyst in Atlanta—much like the other participants—it all feels familiar. I see Calvin, the longtime Show Pro staffer who is always there at 6 a.m. or earlier. A few production assistants are busy tinkering with switches at the front of house. The lighting specialist, Christian Hahn, is checking the transitions he's carefully programmed into the board. Even the furniture in the green room is assembled as I remember it.

But things are different. I am different.

As the special evening session begins, I take my spot in the "mosh pit" with a crowd of other attendees at the foot of the stage. Matt Redman is leading worship, and my hands spring up in adoration of God and what He has done. Matt looks down and we make eye contact. He smiles, and I smile back.

What a difference a year makes.

JIM DALY ON SUCCESSION

JIM DALY IS PRESIDENT AND CEO OF FOCUS ON THE FAMILY.

It's never too early to think about succession. Be intentional, and fight the urge to put it off. As leaders age, they should determine a timeline for succession and increase their activity toward identifying, mentoring, and promoting potential successors. When it is time to let go, they should hand it over cleanly without interference.

At Focus, we have tried to approach succession in a posture of humility by taking the following three steps:

- Identifying people who can move into greater responsibility at all levels. We always have a list of about twenty staff members to be considered for development.
- Identifying and developing potential successors to me. I work alongside the board on this one. We keep a short list of candidates, and we update the list once a year.
- Creating a culture of mentoring. We assign people to mentors and have them meet once a month or more to develop their understanding of the organization. I even have a staff person travel with me to observe, be present, and discuss issues.

This requires a lot of humility. Remember, Christian leadership is engulfed by humility. If you claim to be a Christian leader but do not have humility, then you are simply a leader, not a Christian leader. Humility is what defines the Christian life. At Focus, we hope we're approaching the process of succession in a spirit of humility.

THE HARD WORK OF LEADERSHIP

What has been the most difficult part of being a leader for you personally?

FROM MARK BATTERSON

There is no off switch :).

Some of that is self-inflicted. But it's tough to turn off your brain. Everybody wants a piece of you, which you want to give. But it's tough to maintain margins, and maintain boundaries. It's tough, as Stephen Covey said, to keep first things first. It's a constant battle to stay focused.

FROM CRAIG GROESCHEL

Whenever people ask me how they can pray, I always ask for wisdom. Making the right and wise decisions is probably the biggest challenge I face.

FROM JEFF SLOBOTSKI

Balancing and prioritizing the demands and requests for my time. There's no way that I can get back to everyone who reaches out to me for help, and over time that's been hard for me to realize, as well as share that with others by having to tell many people "no" [for] the sake of my own time, and sanity!

FROM JIM DALY

Changing the existing culture of an organization to something new is a difficult task. Doable, but difficult.

FROM JEREMY COWART

Long-term focus. I'm good at launching the new, shiny idea. But then I'm on to the next idea while the team stays back and has to focus on the long-term. I have to get better at the long-term focus and strategy.

FROM AMENA BROWN OWEN

The most difficult thing during my leadership journey has been learning to not just lead in organizations and in business, but also to make sure I was living a life outside of that. For years as a leader, I put most of my energy and time into the organizations I worked with and realized I didn't have a life. I didn't have relationships or dreams that I enjoyed outside of the leadership positions I held. I needed to take care of myself, but also to enjoy all of the life that was happening around me. I realize that any art I create will come out of the life I live.

FROM SAM RODRIGUEZ

Learning to hold on is equally as important as knowing when to let go. Having the maturity and discernment to distinguish between those individuals God brings into our lives for a season and those he brings for a lifetime.

FROM CARLOS WHITTAKER

Probably leading through personal crisis. We will all hit them at one point or many in our lives. Crisis. I think this is where true leadership will rise. What happens when it all falls apart? How will we respond? I think the answer to this question is going to be created when we are *not* in crisis. How are we developing habits that will transcend our emotions? How are we developing habits that will transcend our limits? The worst time to prepare for crisis is in crisis. As a leader, you will have to lead through a personal crisis or the crisis of another. The daily habits you build will go into cruise control at that point. And that is why *daily* leadership development and books like this are vital to ingest on a constant basis.

FROM JEFF SHINABARGER

Making decisions. As a leader we are put into moments of tension and transition every day, with expectations of knowing what to do, while actually having no idea what to do. So, what do you do when you don't know what to do? This is a question I am continually challenged by as a leader. This tension is heightened when people's lives are dependent on your decisions. When people are impacted, it's difficult.

FROM RYAN O'NEAL

Learning when to say no is very difficult for me, but I recognize the importance of it. Also, I'm an introvert who is still learning how to function well as an extrovert when I need to. So for me, it's a matter of getting my head in the right place.

FROM SCOTT HARRISON

Stress. The responsibility of a rapidly growing organization with massive financial commitments both here at home and abroad, weighs heavy sometimes.

One of my biggest personal challenges has been my aversion to conflict. I'm a peacemaker, and naturally just want everyone to get along. I've had to work hard to run *toward* conflict, have hard conversations, and deal with tense issues in a timely manner. A young friend of mine who leads a $15B company told me that he loves eating hard conversations "for breakfast" . . . That stuck with me.

FROM TODD AND SUSAN PETERSON

Saying no to what I'm supposed to say no to so I'm in a position to say yes to those things I'm to say yes to. Staying humble and not thinking more highly of myself than I ought as acclaim and recognition come over time.

FROM JULIA IMMONEN

As a visionary and also an attention to detail person, I get bogged down with the in-between stuff which isn't my gifting. I've had to learn to release and delegate. Be proactive rather than reactive. I used to let my in-box dictate the course of my day, which was overwhelming and I wondered why I never got my to-do list done. Working that first and attacking my priorities has been so helpful.

FROM KRISTIAN STANFILL

Leadership is not an easy thing mainly because we are leading people, and people are messy. We all have expectations, opinions, insecurities, baggage, worries, fears, questions, and on and on. How do we manage the expectations of our team and lead people through their questions and into clarity? How do we handle a situation when one of our team doesn't agree with a decision that's been made? These are the fires of young leadership and we have to go through them. Go face the issues, have the hard conversation, and learn from the tension and ask for help! Find one or two older, more experienced leaders and keep their number on speed dial. Don't be afraid to reach out and say, "hey, I have an issue here and I have no idea where to start." Don't lead on an island. If you do this you will be the one on someone else's speed dial in five years.

FROM DAVE LOMAS

Criticism. Hands down.

FROM SCOTT DREW

Balancing being a good father and spending quality time with my own family and yet being able to meet the responsibilities and hours required in my coaching job. Be a servant. Jesus came to serve and not be served. If you're serving others you'll always be worthy of leadership and responsibility.

FROM CASS LANGTON

The most difficult parts of being a leader have been: Facing my own shortcomings and then attempting to improve upon them so that I don't limit the team I lead. Allowing other people to do what I personally love to do, in order to develop them into who they are meant to become. Learning to trust God that He has placed me in this leadership position and therefore I should be confident in trusting myself and my "gut feel." Guard your heart, grow your capacity, be generous with your praise, and work hard.

FROM CHAD VEACH

Dealing with relationships that go south. A falling-out, an offense, or betrayal—anything along those lines.

FROM CHRISTINE CAINE

Personally learning to die to self daily. The less of me there is, the more that God can flow through me. Crucifying my flesh is *painful*.

Like Paul "I must die daily."

FROM JENNI CATRON

The most difficult part of leadership for me . . . is *me*. I become easily discouraged by my own inadequacies and insecurities as a leader. I believe wholeheartedly that we must lead ourselves well to lead others better. Self-leadership is a discipline that requires getting honest feedback from those closest to me, humbling myself to admit my weaknesses and passionately pursuing the things that will make me a better leader.

FROM TIM ELMORE

The most difficult problem is continuing in the basics when they lose their novelty. Like a good house, leadership foundations can be a bit boring, but they are fundamental to the longevity of a house. I tend to want to move on past some basic spiritual disciplines, but I must continue in them. The walls only stand if the foundation is strong.

FROM DAN ROCKWELL

Trusting God is first. Trusting myself is trusting that God has a place and purpose for my life. It means I matter because God made me to matter.

Engage in self-reflection. The former CEO of Southwest Airlines brought that home to me when he told me the thing he most enjoyed telling leaders is "know yourself." We can't know who we are apart from self-reflection. The idea that I could be wrong comes from Bob Sutton. I read his book *Scaling Up Excellence* and talked with him about the importance of staying open by saying, "I could be wrong."

The most difficult transition of leadership is from focusing on me versus focusing on others. Letting go of arrogance and trusting the talent, strengths, and perspective of others still challenges me. I often write people off too quickly if they don't meet my expectations or standards. When this happens, I limit them and myself. Leadership is never done in isolation.

FROM SIMON SINEK

Leadership is difficult. Leadership is a responsibility, not a rank. The thing that comes as a shock to most leaders, I think, is just how hard it is. It's like trading in the bachelor life for parenthood. The responsibilities go up, the time and energy we need to commit to the lives and care of others skyrockets, and the rewards of our hard work are no longer our own; they now belong to those we hope to see grow.

Most people fancy being leaders for all the perks and benefits they are afforded. And those are great and they are absolutely there. However, most don't expect that good leadership means they may have to do things against their interests when it would benefit the lives of those in their charge.

FROM PROPAGANDA

Accepting and discerning the weight of my platform. There are times I feel no one is actually listening and following me so I'm not even thinking as a leader, Then I get quickly reminded when I speak too freely and actually see I have a great responsibility. Always leave a person better than you found them. At some point no one will care to hear what you have to say, so use the time you have now to make the greatest impact and have the largest effect.

FROM CHARLES LEE

Practicing what you preach. It's so much easier to talk about good leadership. It's another story to actually live it out. Holding yourself up to the standards you hold others to will continue to be an ongoing struggle. I suppose this struggle is a good thing since it keeps us humble.

One piece of advice that I have truly treasured is in regards to not getting distracted with nonessential tasks or activities in the midst of focusing in on work. I find I'm not naturally created to go in depth on anything that needs my leadership attention while simultaneously being distracted by other demands. Turning things off like e-mails, social [media], etc., have made a world of difference in me becoming a better leader who actually gets things done at the depth and quality our work deserves.

FROM PETE WILSON

The pressure of knowing that my decisions impact others. I hate hurting others and yet I know part of being a leader is that I'm not always going to get it right. And when I don't, people get hurt. I need to own that, confess that, and then move on seeking to get it right next time around.

FROM BRIAN WURZELL

The most difficult part of being a leader, for me, is to keep in priority the cultivation of leading my own life well. Developing an appetite for spiritual disciplines within a *full* schedule/calendar, learning how to say *yes* to the right things and not everything, and leading the things I've been given by healthy example. Lots of work to do in my own life.

FROM HENRY CLOUD

Limiting what I do so that I do not pull people in too many directions. I tend to be a generator of ideas, opportunities, directions, etc., and often think up more than we can do, thereby having a tendency to get people feeling like they are pulled in too many directions. That is one reason to focus on attending, inhibiting, and remembering. I have to always make sure that priorities are in line with expenditures of energy and activity.

FROM JON GORDON

The most difficult part is moving from me to we. Every bone in my body wants to focus on me, but I realize I'm at my best leading others when I focus on *we*. It's overcoming the busyness and stress that causes me to focus on my own survival and make sure I'm spending time serving my family and helping others thrive. Love, serve, and care.

FROM JEFF HENDERSON

I am the most difficult person I lead.

FROM BOBBY GRUENEWALD

Patience. I tend to want to see things happen quickly, but sometimes development needs to take place first. A team or individual might need to grow in their skills or capacity, relationships might need to be invested in, or trust might need to be built between teams. All of this takes time. I've had to learn how to balance patience with being effective at driving results.

FROM JOEL A'BELL

The most difficult part of being a leader these days is simply managing the different ideals, expectations and values we all have as leaders. At high levels of maturity, those things that are right and wrong are usually preferences and convictions of freedom.

NOTES

0 | Let the Transformation Begin

1. Charles Duhigg, *The Power of Habit: Why We Do What We Do in Life and Business* (New York: Random House, 2012), xvi.

2. Ibid., 78–79.

3. Ibid., 88–89.

4. Patty Azzarello, "Your Company's Worst Habits and How to Fix Them," *Fast Company*, April 1, 2013, http://www.fastcompany. com/3006961/your-companys-worst-habits-and-how-fix-them.

5. Jeremy Dean, *Making Habits, Breaking Habits: Why We Do Things, Why We Don't, and How to Make Any Change Stick* (Boston: De Capo, 2013), 6–7.

6. Ann Voskamp, "How to Cultivate the Habit of Focus . . . in an Age of Distraction," *A Holy Experience* (blog), September 5, 2012, http://www.aholyexperience.com/2012/09/ how-to-cultivate-the-habit-of-focus-in-an-age-of-distraction/.

7. Nadia Goodman, "How to Make Good Habits Stick," *Entrepreneur*, July 27, 2012, http://www.entrepreneur.com/blog/224079.

1 | A Habit of Self-Discovery

1. Rick Warren, "Identity Crisis: Just Be You," May 21, 2014, Daily Hope with Rick Warren, http://rickwarren.org/devotional/english/identity-crisis-just-be-you#.U54nCRb6dbw.

2. Ibid.

3. *Oxford Review* (July/August 1993).

2 | A Habit of Openness

1. Kevin Kruse, "What Is Authentic Leadership?" *Forbes*, May 12, 2013, http://www.forbes.com/sites/kevinkruse/2013/05/12/what-is-authentic-leadership/.

2. Ashley Lutz, "Domino's Is Suddenly the World's Hottest Pizza Chain," *Business Insider*, October 23, 2014, http://www.businessinsider.com/dominos-turnaround-story-2014-10.

3. http://www.edelman.com/news/trust-in-government-plunges-to-historic-low.

4. John Maxwell, "Reflections on Leadership," *PM Ministries Newsletter*, June 16, 2004, http://www.preachit.org/newsletter.cfm?record=92&mode=117.

5. Jane Shure, "Leadership Advice: Just Be Yourself," *Huffington Post* (Women), *The Blog*, October 25, 2011, http://www.huffingtonpost.com/jane-shure/leadership-advice_b_1029695.html.

3 | A Habit of Meekness

1. Victor Lipman, "It's Not About You (The Best Leaders Focus on Others)," *Forbes*, September 17, 2012, http://www.forbes.com/sites/victorlipman/2012/09/17/its-not-about-you-the-best-leaders-focus-on-others/.

2. Zuri Berry, "Coughlin: 'Humble enough to prepare, confident enough to perform,'" Boston.com, February 3, 2012, http://www.boston.com/sports/football/patriots/extra_points/2012/02/coughlin_humble.html.

4 | A Habit of Conviction

1. Amber Elliott, "'Runway' winner and Lake Jackson native fashion model shares her style secrets," *Houston Chronicle*, May 2, 2014, http://www.chron.com/life/style/article/Runway-winner-and-Lake-Jackson-native-fashion-5449204.php#photo-6251070.
2. Kalyn Hemphill, "About Me," official website of Kalyn Hemphill, accessed March 12, 2015, http://www.kalynhemphill.com/?page_id=2.
3. Maya Albanese, "How She Leads: Hannah Jones of Nike," *Green Biz* (blog), February 6, 2012, http://www.greenbiz.com/blog/2012/02/06/how-she-leads-hannah-jones-nike.

5 | A Habit of Faith

1. Brennan Manning, *The Furious Longing for God* (Colorado Springs: David C. Cook, 2009), 126.

6 | A Habit of Assignment

1. Anya Kamanetz, "The Four-Year Career," *Fast Company*, January 12, 2012, http://www.fastcompany.com/1802731/four-year-career.

7 | A Habit of Ambition

1. https://www.stephencovey.com/7habits/7habits-habit2.php.
2. https://leadership101.wordpress.com/tag/zig-ziglar/.
3. Kevin Allen, "What True Ambition Really Looks Like," *Fast Company*, May 13, 2014, http://www.fastcompany.com/3030510/what-true-ambition-really-looks-like.

8 | A Habit of Curiosity

1. John Wooden, *Wooden on Leadership* (McGraw Hill, 2005).
2. Gerard Seijts, "Good Leaders Never Stop Learning," *Ivey Business Journal*, July/August 2013, http://iveybusinessjournal.com/topics/leadership/good-leaders-never-stop-learning#.VBC0BEv6dbw.

3. Bill Taylor, "The Best Leaders Are Insatiable Learners," *Harvard Business Review*, September 4, 2014, http://blogs.hbr.org/2014/09/the-best-leaders-are-insatiable-learners/.

4. See the full transcript at http://www.pbs.org/johngardner/sections/writings_speech_1.html.

9 | A Habit of Passion

1. See Robert E. Boyatzis, Annie McKee, and Daniel Goleman, "Reawakening Your Passion for Work," April 2002, *Harvard Business Review*, https://hbr.org/2002/04/reawakening-your-passion-for-work/ar/1.

2. Laura Vanderkam, "6 Ways to Fall in Love with Your Job All Over Again," *Fast Company*, February 14, 2014, http://www.fastcompany.com/3026381/work-smart/6-ways-to-fall-in-love-with-your-job-all-over-again.

3. See also Sebastian Klein, "The Secrets to Career Contentment: Don't Follow Your Passion," *Fast Company*, February 12, 2014, http://www.fastcompany.com/3026272/leadership-now/the-secrets-to-career-contentment-dont-follow-your-passion.

10 | A Habit of Innovation

1. Lydia Dishman, "Social Media Doesn't Sleep," *Fast Company*, March 7, 2014, http://www.fastcompany.com/3027240/innovation-agents/social-media-doesnt-sleep-how-this-local-shop-cranked-sales-from-63k-to-7-.

11 | A Habit of Inspiration

1. James N. Kouzes and Barry Z. Posner, *The Leadership Challenge* (Jossey-Bass, 2012).

2. Dan Rockwell, "The Seven Qualities of Visionary Leaders," *Leadership Freak*, July 23, 2013, https://leadershipfreak.wordpress.com/2013/07/23/the-seven-qualities-of-visionary-leaders/.

3. Dallas Willard

4. Jessica Leber, "This City Lost 1 Million Pounds—Now It's Redesigning Itself to Keep Them Off," *Co.Exist*, September 24, 2014, http://www.fastcoexist.com/3035899/this-city-lost-1-million-pounds-now-its-redesigning-itself-to-keep-them-off.

13 | A Habit of Excellence

1. David Daum, "3 Keys to Business Excellence," *Inc.* magazine, March 12, 2013, *http://www.inc.com/kevin-daum/3-keys-to-business-excellence.html*.
2. Ed Catmull, *Creativity, Inc.* (Random House, 2014).

14 | A Habit of Stick-with-it-ness

1. Harvey Mackay, "The Un-Cool Virtue That Defines Entrepreneurs," *Inc.*, March 20, 2012, http://www.inc.com/harvey-mackay/discipline-defines-great%20entrepreneurs.html.

16 | A Habit of Team Building

1. Conversation with Google employee, July 28, 2014.
2. From his speech at the ELEO Conference in 2014.
3. From Grant Hill interview on *Oprah's Master Class*.

17 | A Habit of Partnership

1. Twyla Tharp, *The Collaborative Habit: Life Lessons for Working Together* (New York: Simon & Schuster, 2009), 11.
2. Ibid., 12.
3. Bob Mudge, "Why Collaboration Is Crucial to Success," *Fast Company*, January 2, 2014, http://www.fastcompany.com/3024246/leadership-now/why-collaboration-is-crucial-to-success.
4. Tharp, *The Collaborative Habit*, 10.

18 | A Habit of Margin

1. Laura Boggess, "Reclaiming Sabbath Keeping: More Than Rest," *The High Calling* (blog), May 18, 2014, http://www.thehighcalling. org/faith/reclaiming-sabbath-keeping-more-rest#.VQLtBY7F_To.

19 | A Habit of Generosity

1. Erika Andersen, "Generous Leaders Aren't Naïve— They're Confident," *Forbes*, July 30, 2012, http:// www.forbes.com/sites/erikaandersen/2012/07/30/ generous-leaders-arent-naive-theyre-confident/.

2. Adam Grant, *Give and Take: A Revolutionary Approach to Success* (New York: Viking, 2013), 4.

3. From a speech at the Leadercast Conference 2014.

20 | A Habit of Succession

1. Jennifer Reingold, "How Home Depot CEO Frank Blake Kept His Legacy from Being Hacked," *Fortune*, October 29, 2014, http://fortune.com/2014/10/29/ home-depot-cybersecurity-reputation-frank-blake/.

ACKNOWLEDGMENTS

As with any book, and for that matter any project in life, the people who help you get to the finish line are of utmost importance. Accordingly, I'd like to offer my deepest gratitude to the following people for being on the journey with me:

First of all, to my parents, Penny and Jerry. For inspiring me to pursue greatness and modeling H3 Leadership. I stand now on a firm foundation because of your love, influence, and impact on my life. Thank you!

To my brother, Brian, and sister-in-law, Jody. Your encouragement and support has been priceless. Adam, Carlee and Jake: I love you and am so proud of you. You each add such flavor to the family, and to my life.

To the Catalyst team for co-laboring together over many years to impact leaders.

To Tyler Reagin for taking the mantle of leadership at Catalyst and running with it. Well done friend!

To Keith Wilmot for allowing me to transition well into this new season of assignment.

To Steve Cockram for walking with me through an incredibly

important season of life, and steering me in the right direction. You're a great coach and friend.

To Jonathan Merritt, for helping craft and create this project. Your help and partnership on this book has been monumental. Grateful for your involvement.

To my pastors Louie and Shelley Giglio, grateful for your encouragement and friendship. And to the Passion City Church staff, love being a part of the house and family. Come on, hello, retweet and bring it!

To Chris Ferebee, a great literary agent and a great friend. Thanks for being an advocate, advisor, guide, counselor and mentor. Can we now consider our work a "library" two books in? Let's keep going.

To Jason Locy and Fivestone for your creative input on this project and a powerful book cover.

To Ben Habeck and the entire team at Dime for helping make life so much easier by providing much needed accounting and tax services for me and BLINC, which frees me up to focus on what I do best.

To Mack Kitchel and the Heystac team for making things not only look good online, but actually work!

To Heather Skelton and Kristen Parrish for bringing skill, much patience, such great insight into the editorial process.

To Joel Miller and Brian Hampton for believing in this project and believing in leaders and the power of influence.

To Katy Boatman for helping market, promote, and make the entire world aware of this book and the message behind it and for putting up with my constant new ideas!

To Tiffany Sawyer for carrying the public relations responsibility. And Beth Gebhard and Heather Adams from Choice Publicity for sharing the message of H3 Leadership into new and expanding markets.

To the entire HarperCollins and Thomas Nelson team. I'm truly honored to get to serve alongside each of you in impacting and equipping leaders.

ABOUT THE AUTHOR

Brad Lomenick is a strategic advisor and leadership consultant specializing in influence, innovation, generational issues, and business strategy. He is a sought-after speaker at conferences, churches, and colleges as well as author of *The Catalyst Leader* (Thomas Nelson, 2013). For over a decade he served as lead visionary and president of Catalyst, one of America's largest movements of Christian leaders. Under his watch Catalyst convened hundreds of thousands of influencers through high-energy and experiential leadership conferences across the United States.

Before running Catalyst, he spent five years involved in the growth of the nationally acclaimed *Life@Work* magazine and was a management consultant with Cornerstone Group, where he worked with a variety of companies, organizations, and nonprofit enterprises. Before that, he served as foreman for Lost Valley Ranch, a four-diamond working guest ranch in the mountains of Colorado.

He has had the privilege of interviewing and interacting with dozens of the world's leading thinkers—including Malcolm Gladwell, Jim Collins, Seth Godin, Marcus Buckingham, Jack

Dorsey, Simon Sinek, Patrick Lencioni, Mark Burnett, Tony Dungy, Dave Ramsey, Rick Warren, Brene Brown, and more. Brad has been featured in notable outlets such as *TIME*, *Atlanta Journal Constitution*, and *Fast Company*.

Brad serves on the advisory boards for Suffered Enough, the A21 Campaign, Red Eye Inc., and Praxis. He holds a bachelor's degree from the University of Oklahoma and currently resides outside of Atlanta.

Follow him on Twitter, LinkedIn, Instagram, and Facebook: @bradlomenick

Check out his blog: www.BradLomenick.com